Why Wait till Sunday?

Why Wait till Sunday?

An Action Approach to Local Evangelism

HOLLIS L. GREEN

GlobalEdAdvancePress
www.gea-books.com

WHY WAIT TILL SUNDAY?

Copyright © 1975, 2012 by Hollis L. Green

Library of Congress Control Number: 2012953173

Why Wait Till Sunday?

ISBN 978-1-935434-27-6

Subject Codes and Description: 1. REL108010 Religion: Christian Church - Growth 2. REL014520 Religion: Christian Church – Administration: Program Resources 3. REL012120 Religion: Christian Life – Spiritual Growth

All rights reserved, including the right to reproduce this book or any part thereof in any form, except for inclusion of brief quotations in a review, without the written permission of the author and GlobalEdAdvance Press.

Printed in Australia, Brazil, France, Germany, Italy, Spain, UK, and USA.

The Press does not have ownership of the contents of a book; this is the author's work and the author owns the copyright. All theory, concepts, constructs, and perspectives are those of the author and not necessarily the Press. They are presented for open and free discussion of the issues involved. All comments and feedback should be directed to the Email: [comments4author@aol.com] and the comments will be forwarded to the author for response.

First Edition (1975) published by Bethany Fellowship, Inc.

This Edition (2012) published by:

GlobalEdAdvance Press
www.gea-books.com

DEDICATED TO

Dr. David P. Haney

Who pioneered small group efforts for the SBC.

~

Preface to this Edition

As churches continue to weaken and some actually fail, a plan for renewal is needed now more than ever. This book provides a way for the pastor of a small church to mobilize fifty (50) people into Action Groups to work toward renewal and growth. This plan becomes an alliance for evangelism outreach and a way to re-enlist the negligent. Seven (7) groups of (7) work with the pastor in bring up ideas from the people in a spiritual use of a "brainstorming" effort to provide new ways and means of advancing the local church.

This book is an outgrowth of the classic Evangelism and Church Growth book, *Why Churches Die*, and becomes part of the evangelism/church growth series by Hollis L. Green, ThD, PhD.

1. **Why Churches Die** –A guide to basic evangelism and church growth. ISBN 978-0-9796019-0-3
2. **Why Wait till Sunday?** –A workable plan for local church evangelism and renewal ISBN 978-1-935434–27-6
3. **Why Christianity Fails** – An effort to make Christianity viable in the Twenty-first century ISBN 978-0-9796019-1-0
4. **Titanic Lessons** –Do historic realities predict problems for a growing Church? ISBN 9788-0-9796019-6-5
5. **Discipleship** – A vital aspect of Christian living ISBN 978-0-9796019-5-8
6. **Fighting the Amalekites** – A guide to spiritual warfare. ISBN 978-9-9796019-2-7
7. **Interpreting an Author's Words** –Improving a pastor's study and writing skills. ISBN 978-0-9801674-7-4

8. **Sympathetic Leadership Cybernetics** – Serving organizations through Shepherd Management & Servant Leadership ISBN 978-1-935434-52-8

9. **Transformational Leadership in Education**: Strengths-based approach to change for Administrators, Teachers & Guidance Counselors ISBN 978-0-9801674-6-7

10. **The EVERGREEN Devotional New Testament: Complete Edition** – A candid rendering of the New Testament in chronological order by books.
    ISBN 978-1-935434-26-9

~

Other books by Hollis Lynn Green may be found at the site *www.gea-books.com* or other Internet sites; such as, Amazon, Barnes & Nobel, etc.

Foreword

"Evangelism" is a color word in twentieth-century Christianity: a divisive issue. It wasn't in New Testament times. And, it shouldn't be today. Jesus left little room for doubt. His first recorded command ("Let your light shine") and His last recorded, as well ("You are to be witnesses"), both point to our continuing assignment. As Elton Trueblood said, "A nonwitnessing Christian is a contradiction in terms."

But for those committed to His command, the next question is "How?" Hollis Green's *Why Wait Till Sunday?* is an answer. Tried and tested, he gives us a workable plan for local church evangelism. I liked it immediately because it contained some of the ideas in my own *Renew My Church, The Idea of the Laity,* and *Breakthrough into Renewal,* as well as some of things Reid Hardin and I are seeking to accomplish through our "Journey into Life-style Evangelism and Ministry" strategy among Southern Baptists.

But, even more so, I like it because all the essential elements are present: the pastor in his rightful role; the laity in their full-fledged capacities; the church in proper, central focus; and the lost, unfulfilled people in this world as the prime concern.

You can't beat that for being New Testament—whether in the first or the twentieth century!

> David P. Haney
> Director of Lay Renewal
> Brotherhood Commission
> Southern Baptist Convention

Preface

The primary effect of reading about evangelism is to awaken, not inform. Unless words, concepts, sentences, or paragraphs explode beneficently and creatively, revealing life as it is and suggesting changes for the better, reading is a waste of time. What is read must be assimilated. The recently converted Chinese who once wrote, "I am now reading the Bible and *behaving* it," caught the import and basic principle of assimilative Bible study. We cannot just read and believe. We must read and BEHAVE! The same is true of this book.

Evangelism is an exciting aspect of the Christian life. It is the work of every believer. Each Christian is an "evangelist" with a little "e" and a "missionary" with a little "m." Evangelism is the work of Christian laity, not the exclusive prerogative of the clergy. The layman may not be called as a "baptizer," but he is certainly sent as a "gospelizer." The pastor has his privileges and responsibilities, but this in no way requires a forfeit of lay ministry by the congregation.

In the charge to Timothy, Paul made it clear that Timothy as a preacher was to preach the Word at all times and under all conditions. Sound doctrine was to be his concern; nevertheless, in addition to all his responsibilities as a preacher, Timothy was told to do the "work of an evangelist." Only by continuing to be a Christian concerned with evangelism every day everywhere could he fulfill his ministry. The pastor is still a Christian layman—in fact, he is the chief layman and should set the pace and pattern for the entire congregation. He can do the work of only one man. The whole church must be mobilized. This is the purpose of an Alliance for Evangelism.

An Alliance for Evangelism seeks "doers of the Word." Too often Christians only hear the sound of the sermon and never really listen to the meaning of the message. The time has come for action in the area of personal evangelism; time for preachers and Christians everywhere to get involved in a daily ministry for souls. When personal evangelism works, the church will enjoy total mobilization—total evangelism.

This plan of action works. It has been tested and results were gratifying. There is a secret which causes this plan to work: in addition to prayer, personal study and preaching the pastor must place priority on evangelism. The pastor is the key. He must place the Alliance for Evangelism on his list of personal priorities. Why not? Pastors have tried every conceivable approach. It is time to let the people of the church in on solving the problems of evangelism. Why not drop a few activities or time-consuming programs that are not working and place priority on this action approach to local evangelism and church growth? A program of the people, by the people, and for personal evangelism is a people-to-people effort. It works all week. Why wait till Sunday?

Hollis L. Green, Th.D.
Jacksonville, Florida

Contents

Foreword 7
Preface 9
Quick Start Action 17

I. A FRESH APPRAISAL OF LOCAL
   CHURCH VITALITY 21
   1. A "Wait Till Sunday" Attitude
   2. An Abuse of Sacred Trust
   3. The Basic Method of Outreach
   4. The Growing Churches of America
   5. The Seeds of Failure
   6. A Word of Caution
   7. A Personal Ministry for Souls
   8. An Upsurge of Awareness
   9. A People-to-People Effort
   10. An Alliance of Believers
   11. A Church Project
   12. A Personalized Program
   13. A New Testament Way
   14. A Candidate for Salvation
   15. The Joy of Seeing Converts

II. A SOLUTION FOR UPWARD
    DELEGATION 33
    16. Technique of a Finished Task
    17. Development of Self-sufficiency

18. Proper Division of Labor
19. Program of Evangelism
20. Leadership by Default
21. Vested Interest of Leaders
22. Leadership by Previous Pattern
23. Principles of Learning
24. Key to Adult Learning

III. AN ACTION APPROACH TO
INDIVIDUAL CHANGE.................. 41
25. Opinion of Self
26. Perception of Others
27. Action Effect on Attitudes
28. Pattern of Interlocking Attitudes
29. Reason for Failure
30. System of Behavior
31. Change in Attitude
32. Build on Background
33. Begin with Concern
34. Source of Creative Thinking
35. Protection for Creative People
36. Freedom of Expression
37. Freshness of Perception
38. Obstacles in the Mind
39. Plenty of Ideas
40. Shock of Total Program
41. Process of Individual Narrowing
42. Choking Underbrush of Programs
43. Problem of "How To"

IV. A TASK FORCE FOR
PERSONAL INVOLVEMENT............. 53
44. A Spirit of *Koinonia*
45. An Opportunity for Lay Participation
46. A Spirit of Cooperation
47. A Task Force Project
48. A Local Problem-Solving Effort

49. A Coordinating Council
50. A Six-Month Calendar
51. A Back-Up Relationship
52. A Guide to Innovative Activity
53. A Personal Talk-Sheet
54. A Summary Report
55. Action Group Goals
56. An Agenda for Discussion
57. A Multiplicity of Ideas

V. A SEARCH FOR INNOVATIVE IDEAS 65
58. Selecting Action Group Leaders
59. Preparing Action Group Leaders
60. Three Sessions of Training
61. Background of Discussion Experience
62. Groups Encourage Creativity
63. Excellent Background Experience
64. Adequate Meeting Place
65. Feeling of Togetherness Needed
66. Clear Objectives Necessary
67. Participant Part of the Problem
68. Many Possible Solutions
69. Opinions Usually Differ
70. Unprejudicial Search for Solutions
71. Elicit Creative Ideas
72. Accept Rather Than Reject Ideas
73. Reflect Participant's View
74. Clarify and Rephrase Statements
75. Use Hitchhiking
76. Silence Sparks Creativity
77. Learn by Listening
78. Levels of Mental Activity
79. Springboards to Discussion
80. Method of Stimulating Discussion
81. Action Group Resource
82. Program-Centered Concerns
83. Personnel-Centered Concerns

84. Organization-Centered Concerns
85. Fellowship-Centered Concerns
86. Renewal-Centered Concerns

VI. A FORUM FOR LAY EXPRESSION 81
87. Participation in an Action Group
88. Problem of Unused Abilities
89. A Secret of Happiness
90. A Sequence of Events
91. Achievement of Maximum Usefulness
92. Achievement Begins with Dissatisfaction
93. An Amazing Part of Idea Gathering
94. Available Solutions for Evangelism
95. A Forum for Expression
96. A Spoke in the Wheel
97. Speak with Confidence
98. Listen to Others
99. A Process of Understanding
100. Stick to the Point
101. Concentration on the Moment
102. Self-interest Limits Contribution
103. Attitudes of Participants
104. Evaluation of Participation
105. Implementation of Ideas

VII. A PROCESS OF SUMMARY
REPORTING 93
106. Choosing Action Group Secretaries
107. An Orientation Session for Secretaries
108. A Most Important Role
109. Conscientious and Efficient Function
110. Meeting Arrangements
111. Members of the Same Team
112. Note-Taking and Reports

VIII. AN IMPLEMENTATION OF
LOCAL SOLUTIONS 99
113. Personnel for TASK FORCE TWO

114. Procedure of Classifying
  115. Report in Three Parts
  116. Use of Reports
  117. Burden of Implementation
APPENDICES............................ 103
  A. Alliance for Evangelism Timetable
  B. Evaluation Worksheet and Guide to Innovative Activity
  C. Action Report
  D. Participant's Pledge
  E. Suggested Reading
  F. Leader's Sequence Orientation

ALLIANCE FOR EVANGELISM

... An "alliance" of believers blended in spiritual harmony and cooperation for the accomplishment of basic New Testament evangelism.

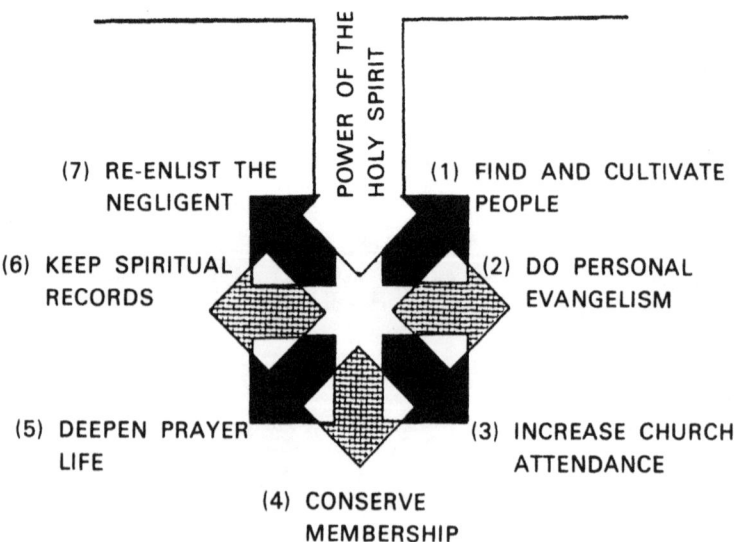

ACTION GROUPS

QUICK START
5 Step S-T-A-R-T Action Approach

1. Study the spiritual condition of your people. What are their personal needs? Are they taking advantage of present opportunities to participate in the church program? Why? Why not? Write your answers.

2. Tabulate the possibilities for action in mobilizing the people for evangelism. What can you do? What can the church staff do? What can be done by agencies and groups of the church? What can individuals do? Write what you can do.

3. Arrange a plan of action. An Alliance for Evangelism is a plan of action already structured to motivate active and creative involvement in local evangelism. *Why Wait Till Sunday?* is based on the concepts and insights developed by Dr. Green in *Why Churches Die*. Begin by reading this book as a resource text (published by Bethany Fellowship, Inc.; available in paperback). Then read *Why Wait Till Sunday?* This text serves as a manual for an Alliance for Evangelism. Use the Leader's Sequence Orientation (Appendix F) and write out a personal plan of action.

4. Recheck the structure and the plan advanced

in the text. Be sure you understand the number of participants needed in Task Force ONE and the purpose and function of the Action Group session, the Coordinating Council, the meetings of the entire Alliance for Evangelism and Task Force TWO. Check the timetable listings for the Church Calendar and the Leader's Sequence Orientation. Mimeograph or quick copy the forms (Appendices B, C, D). Then get started!

5. Take the first step. The best way to start is simply to start. Yet that simple action is often harder than expected. Chances are some may get bogged down in the Department of Utter Confusion, so here are some simple quideposts to an action start. It is a simple 5-step S-T-A-R-T action approach.

1. STUDY the situation, needs, opportunities.
2. TABULATE the possibilities for action.
3. ARRANGE a plan for action.
4. RECHECK the procedure.
5. TAKE the first step—a journey of a thousand miles begins with a single step. So get started. Leave the whys and wherefores and plunge into the positive steps (after much prayer, of course). Remember the key word of an Alliance for Evangelism is A-C-T-I-O-N. This book may change your way of thinking about evangelism, but you must follow the plan of action to change your way of doing evangelism. Behave the New Testament. God is on your side. Seek the guidance of the Holy Spirit. Challenge the church leadership. Act *now!*

ALLIANCE FOR EVANGELISM

...An "alliance" of believers blended in spiritual harmony and cooperation for the accomplishment of basic New Testament evangelism.

I
A Fresh Appraisal of Local Church Vitality

Sunday is important. As the first day, Sunday sets the pace and pattern for Christian involvement in the world. Tragically, Christians have become only church-goers who wait till Sunday to demonstrate spiritual concerns. This is neither a New Testament pattern nor a responsible life-style for Christians. Sure, early believers worshipped on Sunday, but they were also daily involved in the business of "making disciples." They did not wait till Sunday to teach and preach Jesus Christ. They did not wait till Sunday to evangelize. They were daily disciples.

1. A "Wait Till Sunday" Attitude

Local church vitality has waned because of this "wait till Sunday" attitude. This attitude, during the past quarter century, has weakened many congregations and made individual Christians ineffective in their daily lives. Some churches have grown stale, impersonal and unconcerned about the unconverted. While the church was busy with housekeeping chores, preparing next Sunday's sermon, music, bulletin and Sunday school lesson, many individuals in the community became further alienated from the Christian cause. Preoccupied with what was to happen next Sunday, the church lost sight of New Testament involvement in evangelism.

2. An Abuse of Sacred Trust

As attendance and interest waned or failed to grow in proportion to the leader's zeal or ego, some abused their sacred trust by attempting to manipulate growth. Church growth is a natural process. Authentic New Testament growth cannot be mechanically induced; it is the work of the Holy Spirit through dedicated and committed disciples of Christ. Regretfully, in some cases, this deceptive expedient became a religious camouflage to cover a lack of spiritual concern and Christian dedication. Duty to the church was substituted for dedication to Christ. Secular methodology replaced spiritual men. Programs used unwilling people. Yet, in some places it worked. Churches became "successful" and began to reach the community. Miraculously God worked. Revival came. A potentially disastrous charade was transformed by the power of the Holy Spirit into a dedicated congregation on the move for God.

3. The Basic Method of Outreach

Some churches have adequately combined super-aggressive programming with individual spiritual commitment and involvement, while others have tragically missed the spiritual mark. Granted that anything, any effort, any program that wins souls must be considered within the will of God, this in no way excuses the risks involved in substituting machines for men or replacing personal initiative with programs. Men are still God's basic method of outreach. Personal effort by individual Christians remains the most effective tool of evangelism.

4. *The Growing Churches of America*

Imitation is the real problem. Small churches, without the dedication or experience, attempt to copy super-aggressive congregations and fail. Without the biblical background or spiritual foundation that brought the super-church to its place of excellence, most churches are not adequately prepared to make the transition from simple and personalized efforts to the complicated contemporary approach. The growing churches of America have something in common. Their leaders understand the essential balance of four basic New Testament elements: (1) a sound Bible preaching-teaching ministry, (2) a personalized outreach effort for evangelism, (3) an active program of discipleship and convert training, and (4) an emphasis on the ministry and work of the Holy Spirit. If these growing churches are to be imitated, it must begin with this solid foundational balance. Simply copying programs or duplicating themes will not suffice for the essential spiritual foundation required to build a New Testament congregation.

5. *The Seeds of Failure*

Success often contains the seeds of failure. Certainly, the growing income in many churches represents a maturing spiritual awareness; however, growing budgets occasionally reflect an effort by men to buy their way out of personal involvement. Although this is usually an unconscious act, it in no way erases the stain of this reality from the church. Buying one's way out of personal involvement is nothing new; it was a common practice during the Civil War. Then, the rich could buy a substitute or pay a bounty and avoid the national draft. The church must never permit material contribution to be substituted for personal involvement.

6. *A Word of Caution*

Tithes and offerings are certainly God's plan for financing the church. This money supports the ministry and undergirds the outreach of the local church. Yet, the disbursement of these funds and programs of ministry they support are in the hands of chosen members of the congregation. Stewardship is a sacred trust. God's money must be used wisely. A word of caution is in order here. When additional staff is secured for the church, this should in no way relieve others of personal and continued responsibility. The same is true of such programs as the bus ministry. When the church can afford to initiate a bus ministry, it should be clear that a concentrated effort by a few to bring in the underprivileged in no way relieves other Christians from using the back seat of the family car to bring people to the house of God. The preoccupation of some with a superficial missionary zeal (superficial because it shows no concern for souls at home) can prove to be a tragic camouflage for a lack of personal participation in the ongoing program of total evangelism. This in no way decrys the dedicated efforts of many to enlarge the missionary budget, but it is an urgent appeal for a missionary church to assert its responsibility to the lost everywhere.

7. *A Personal Ministry for Souls*

The practical meaning is clear. No one can hire a substitute to do his spiritual work. There is no legitimate way to program the individual out of personal soul winning. Winning souls begins with an individual concerned about others and ends with an individual concerned about himself and his relationship with God. The church needs a growing budget. Additions should be made to the church staff. There ought to be an aggressive outreach ministry. The church must be permeated with missionary zeal. These are legitimate and needed aspects of a growing church, but they must in no way detract from the individual obligation of each and every Christian to be involved in a personal ministry for souls.

8. *An Upsurge of Awareness*

An upsurge of awareness that something must be done to give the local church new vitality in evangelism requires an urgent reappraisal of both the program structure and the participation of individuals in the life of the church. The church, because of past promotional schemes, has been accused of shallowness in its drive for attendance. A fresh look at New Testament evangelism reveals the need for evaluation of the basic outreach program of the church. New concerns must be expressed for enlistment, education, and New Testament growth.

9. *A People-to-People Effort*

The best results in evangelism are produced through a systematic effort; however, it is evident that even spasmodic ventures in people-to-people efforts have proved to be a tremendous growth factor. The active participation of laymen in an organized program of outreach furnishes a church with a new fervor for New Testament evangelism, and an important fact becomes clear: God uses people to carry

His message to the lost. The objective of New Testament evangelism can be easily summarized in one word—*souls!*

10. *An Alliance of Believers*

The church suffers when too few attempt to do too much! This is often the fault of the minister himself. He has not taken the time to train and to employ the capacities of the laity and is thus constantly engaged in tasks which might be better done by the membership. To free the minister for more pressing responsibilities related to his spiritual leadership, to give opportunity for effective lay participation, to knit the church into a closer fellowship, to make possible a better dissemination of evangelism programs and plans to the congregation, the adoption of an Alliance for Evangelism is proposed. The alliance can become an invaluable source of spiritual and organizational strength for the local church. The Alliance for Evangelism is exactly what the names inplies: An alliance of believers blended in spiritual harmony and cooperation for the accomplishment of basic New Testament evangelism. (See Chapter IV for details.)

11. *A Church Project*

Evangelism is a church project, not the sacred task of a select few. Christian fellowship and concern should express itself in house-to-house involvement. The entire church must be motivated to participation. Individual participation and enthusiasm are determined by information and personal involvement.

An effective program must appeal to the drives that cause action. These drives are: desire for social approval, desire to be of service, and desire for

God's approval. When the task is understood and supervised, it can be accomplished. The results will be new life for the church, because scriptural participation produces spiritual enthusiasm. Involving laymen in an active program of evangelism gives a church a new zest for spiritual life and helps to create the concept of concern that translates the language of words about evangelism into a language of relationships that wins friends for Christ and brings them into the fellowship of His church.

12. *A Personalized Program*

The Bible furnishes ample precedent for a personalized persistent program of outreach and growth. Not only do we find an authoritative example in the early church, we are confronted on the contemporary scene with numerous churches that are constantly being strengthened and enlarged through a personalized program of outreach. The challenge is not to maintain the *status quo*, but to reach out by faith to the unchurched multitudes and even to the cloistered church members who have never been mobilized for true Christian involvement.

13. *A New Testament Way*

A true dimension of present growth opportunities comes from a full grasp of the impact and pattern of New Testament evangelism. Personal soul winning was the simple pattern. No one waited until Sunday or invited an individual "to come to church" to hear a sermon to be saved. Every Christian felt he was a priest and constantly presented the claims of the gospel to every man any and everywhere. There is no end to the growth of a church that steps out on faith and concentrates on a central idea—that of everyone going everywhere and sharing the gospel with assurance that the Lord will confirm His Word with spiritual results. This was the valid New Testament way. It is still valid today!

14. *A Candidate for Salvation*

Of course the Sunday music and the message helps, but it is the Spirit who convicts, not the song or the sermon. Since the Holy Spirit has been poured out on all flesh to convict the whole world of sin, of righteousness, and of judgment, it is logical to assume that every person is a candidate for salvation. Such an assumptive attitude greatly increases the believer's self-confidence in personal evangelism. Since Christ died for the whole world and the Spirit convicts the whole world, Christians must see everyone as a prospect. Presenting the claims of Christ, the simple sharing of the good news, must be the work of the whole church.

15. *The Joy of Seeing Converts*

Since evangelism is everyone's business every day, the church must not wait until Sunday to do soul winning. As the opportunity arises, at the earliest point in time, at the greatest distance from the church, the gospel must be shared with anyone who will listen. Christians must go beyond simply inviting people to church. Each believer must become an evangelist everywhere all week long. Thus, those who worship on Sunday and go forth weeping for souls will doubtless return to the church sanctuary bringing with them souls they have led to Christ. They can say, "Follow me as I follow Christ." Great is the joy of seeing such converts make a public profession of their faith on Sunday, request water baptism, and be received into the church fellowship. This is the New Testament way.

The greatest number of soul-winning prospects are in the world, not in the church. The major effort of evangelism should be made out where the sinners are. Some unconverted folk are sure to make their way to the church services seeking a way out of their present plight; these can and must be won. Yet, a great majority of those converted in the church services could have been won earlier. When the unsaved must wait until Sunday for an opportunity to accept Christ, something is missing in the local program of evangelism.

When the unconverted reach the sanctuary unsaved, the program of evangelism is not fully working. Someone who could have won the person to Christ neglected his opportunity and opted to invite the individual to Sunday school or church. He simply waited until Sunday and delegated upwardly his responsibility to the pastor. Why did he feel inadequate to witness? Why did he neglect the obvious opportunity? Perhaps he was unsure of his own relationship with Christ. Maybe he was just a product of the old system that waits until Sunday. He may not have been equipped as a saint to do his work as an evangelist. Regardless of why or how the unconverted reached the sanctuary unsaved, the pastor was asked to do on Sunday what could have been done earlier by anyone sensitive to the leading of the Holy Spirit.

What happens when the church waits until Sunday? How many do not live until Sunday? How many who promise to attend never make it? What if the Lord were to come before Sunday? Christians must not wait. The church should not wait. Evangelism is everyone's work every day, as the Lord leads. This is what evangelism is all about. Otherwise the gathering for worship and fellowship, the singing of hymns and the preaching of the Word will never change the world. Believers must behave the Scriptures. Christians must be "doers of the Word." Followers of Christ must be true disciples, inscripturated and inspired as living epistles of God's power and purpose through the church. Then, Christians will be changed. The whole church will be changed. The whole church will be mobilized for action. Only then can the world be won for Christ. It can never be won with a one-day-a-week operation. Evangelism must become a way of life.

ALLIANCE FOR EVANGELISM

...An "alliance" of believers blended in spiritual harmony and cooperation for the accomplishment of basic New Testament evangelism.

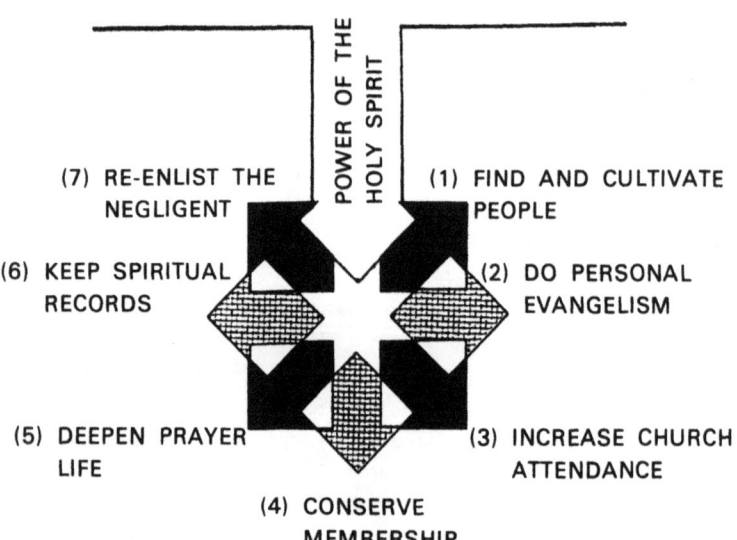

ACTION GROUPS

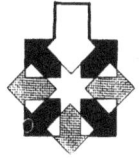

II
A Solution for Upward Delegation

Churches today suffer from the problem of upward delegation. The Great Commission was given to the whole church, and each individual is responsibile for sharing his faith on a daily basis. Yet, some Christians throughout the church are constantly delegating their responsibility upwardly to the pastor or other professional and paid staff members. They simply wait until Sunday, expecting the events of one day to solve all their problems. This greatly handicaps any mobilization effort for evangelism.

16. *Technique of a Finished Task*

Industry solved the problem of upward delegation through the technique of a finished task. The simple solution was for each person to complete his work to the best of his ability without passing the responsibility upwardly. Usually the man on the job is more knowledgeable of the problem than anyone available. Yet, not wishing to assume responsibility for his own action, he constantly seeks the advice and counsel of his superiors concerning various minor problems. This occupies leadership with many unnecessary decisions which could better be made at a lower level. Individuals must understand and assume responsibility for their action before the problem of upward delegation can be solved. This fact has great significance to soul winning. Christians must not wait until Sunday to demonstrate concern for a lost world.

17. *Development of Self-sufficiency*

The church must develop self-sufficient and effective Christians who can personally do their spiritual task with confidence. Since evangelism is everyone's responsibility, each believer must be equipped and prepared to do this work on a daily basis. The church must stop waiting until Sunday, waiting for revival, waiting for a professional evangelist, waiting for the pastor or church staff to perform and do their God-given and scripturally assigned tasks. Each believer must develop his knowledge of the Word of God and a capacity to pray for himself and his needs. Only when the individual can assume responsibility for himself can he be confident in his spiritual mission to reach others.

18. *Proper Division of Labor*

Upward delegation causes an improper division of labor in outreach ministries. This can be solved only by putting everyone to work doing evangelism where he is. The pastor and the few in leadership positions are often bogged down in nonessential and unproductive details. It is necessary for each church to understand that their minister remains in fact a layman: he has Christian lay responsibilities. Yet, he can only do the work of one man and adequately perform his pastoral call. Each layman also has a ministry. There must be a proper division of the evangelism work load. Each Christian has a responsibility to serve his Lord and to share his faith on a daily basis as the opportunity arises. Only when everyone is daily involved can the work load of evangelism be properly distributed.

19. *Program of Evangelism*

Too long the program of evangelism has been sent *down* from the top or brought *in* from outside. It may have been effective elsewhere, but local adaptations and tailoring is not made. When it fails to produce the desired local results, often the people involved feel that they are at fault. This breeds a negative reaction to evangelism and causes some Christians to avoid involvement in vital programs of outreach.

20. *Leadership by Default*

A lack of local initiative and the absence of meaningful lay involvement in the ongoing program of ministry produces a leadership by default. Often those in present leadership did not wish to be there. Tragically, many are not qualified for the position they hold. Yet, their willingness to serve places them in a position of responsibility greater than they can bear with grace and victory. Consequently, a great deal of discouragement exists and sometimes the "discouraging word" is passed to others. Thus, the leadership enlistment program becomes frustrated. Notwithstanding, the church continues to function with inadequate leaders.

21. *Vested Interest of Leaders*

Entrenched leaders, regardless of how or why they arrived at their position of authority, often develop vested interest which further complicates change. They have become comfortable in the way things are handled because the program has been structured to meet their limited capacity. The timetable meets their convenience. Any change would upset the apple cart. Accordingly, they oppose any program innovation or personal initiative which would alter their present position of prestige and power. This vested interest becomes a major obstacle in initiating a new and vital program of evangelism in the local church.

22. *Leadership by Previous Pattern*

Local leadership appears to be walking a treadmill. They are often caught in a prison of previous pattern. Consequently, a great deal of motion without progress becomes a way of life for the congregation. The pastor and his staff are hyperactive, but the church seems to be a sleeping giant. After preliminary efforts to mobilize and motivate the congregation fail, leadership often adjusts to a mediocrity and settles for something less than what the church could be. Adequate leadership training could change this condition by altering the leader's attitudes and the leader's behavior.

23. *Principles of Learning*

When leaders increase their knowledge without changing their behavior, the training failed to accomplish its purpose. Most efforts of leadership training fail because the program did not follow accepted principles of learning as these principles apply to adults. Most efforts assume that participants have developed those basic skills needed by all leaders: how to sort out the facts, make a decision, and work effectively with people. Some accepted principles of adult learning are:

1. Most people must be motivated to put forth the extra effort required to learn (and improve).
2. An open mind is essential to learning.
3. Adults usually filter out new ideas instead of giving them serious consideration.
4. Learning involves change and most adults resist change because they cannot see how the change will help them personally.
5. Adults grow mentally (learn) to the extent they think things through for themselves. A good leader must demonstrate solutions rather than simply giving answers to questions.
6. Usually adults solve a problem by using their past experiences and the information presently available. Adults must feel free to question information and to explore differences of opinion to be satisfied that what he is learning is correct.
7. Adults do not learn by merely storing information. Learning takes place by understanding and practicing correct procedures until they become automatic.

24. *Key to Adult Learning*

The myth that adults cannot learn must be destroyed. The learning rate may decline as adults age, but not the capacity to learn. Current research places emphasis on motivation as the key to learning and change. Older adults may require more motivation or the reactivation of personal concern, but it can be done. This is a vital part of an Alliance for Evangelism. It is impossible to isolate a single motive to produce action in an adult because motivation is a complex process. Adult interests include: personal health, religion, friendship, vocation, politics, aesthetics, economics, and recreation. This list is a key to motivating adult involvement in all of life. Evangelism is a vital part of the Christian way of life and should be an expressed part of adult living. When everyone assumes his personal responsibility, the problem of upward delegation is solved.

ALLIANCE FOR EVANGELISM

...An Action Group process to stimulate creative and innovative solutions to local outreach problems.

ACTION GROUP PROCESS

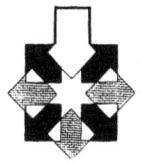

III
An Action Approach to Individual Change

Sometimes leaders do not change because they do not "feel good" about the changes. This necessitates an action approach. Action seems to follow feeling, but really action and feeling go together, and by regulating the action which is under the more direct control of the will, feelings may be indirectly regulated. It is necessary for leaders to practice this action approach. This is essential to his own self-image and an adequate image of leadership in the minds of others.

25. *Opinion of Self*

What a leader does influences others' opinion of him, and from their reaction to his behavior he draws some part of his opinion of himself. Through this interaction he develops an adequate self-image. Provided he is a guiding force, he may be classified a leader. If he only officiates, he may be thought of as simply an officer. Certainly, no leader could be identified as a soul winner unless he actively participated in evangelism.

26. *Perception of Others*

Action by the leader exerts a second effect. His behavior influences his perception of others. Everything he does contributes to this vantage point. If he is not interested in evangelism, he cannot be spiritually interested in people. The effect of vantage point significantly influences prejudice and stops the leader from discovering evidence that would change his attitude toward people or programs. It is important, then, to get the leader to act and to act decisively and systematically. When he acts, he produces a direct effect upon himself. Action changes his attitude toward others.

27. *Action Effect on Attitudes*

Action produces a far more sweeping effect on underlying attitudes than is believed. Action provides the leader with observations of himself. When a decision to act is made, for a time the attitudes that gave rise to that decision are intensified in proportion to the contribution each attitude made. By his actions he can identify the personal motivation that brought about the action. Action provides him with personal observations, and he can judge himself in the same way other people judge him by his actions. He should be taught to use these personal observations in recognizing himself and constructing a picture of reality as it relates to his own self-image. Personal action and significant involvement in evangelism can drastically change a leader's feelings about himself and greatly enhance his leadership.

28. *Pattern of Interlocking Attitudes*

The process of change is slow and difficult. When a leader holds a purely personal attitude for any length of time, he unknowingly reproduces it. In his effort to hold this attitude in place, he generates not a single activity but a multiplicity of acts to support his attitude. Moreover, attitudes can be seldom altered by adopting single practices or by stopping them. It is a complex pattern of interlocking attitudes that does not allow for change of component parts. The whole process must be replaced and a new learning sequence established. Thus, the action approach is necessary to produce meaningful change in the attitudes of people and in the effectiveness of programs.

29. Reason for Failure

Some leaders feel frustrated because they have already attempted to change their underlying attitudes and have failed. The reason for this failure is that they attempted to change the attitude merely by changing their mind. This cannot be done. It must be changed by a series of direct and personal acts which will replace the previous attitude with constructive action. He must attempt to identify the multitude of acts which caused the attitude in the first place and change them systematically. The real problem in the process is that unknowingly he constantly renews old attitudes by present activity. It is important then that leadership constantly evaluate their weekly schedule and daily activities to be certain they are not reinforcing unwanted attitudes or by their own actions teaching by a poor example.

30. System of Behavior

To get rid of unwanted attitudes, a leader must carefully search for the activities by which he is renewing old attitudes. Perhaps he must change his manner of dealing with people and understand his whole system of behavior which has been aggravating the problem and helping to hold the unwanted attitude in place. It is not a single act but perseverance with carefully thought-out patterns of activities that will ultimately purge a leader's mind of negative and unwanted attitudes about progress.

31. *Change in Attitude*

An Alliance for Evangelism is designed to be superimposed on any local church program, as a task force with a basic goal of bringing about a creative and innovative attitude to outreach programming. It will not work by changing minor things about the present program or personnel. It must be an entirely new approach, a practical program coming *up* from the grass roots, rather than a theoretical program coming *down* to the congregation. A change in attitude is more important than a change in program. Enthusiastic and spiritual leaders add the positive punch to most effective programs.

32. *Build on Background*

Churchmen usually think of the mind as a storehouse to be filled when in reality the mind is a resource to be used. In every area in which creative thought or action occurs, the individual builds on his own individual background and heritage. This is important to a local program of evangelism because each individual is different. A variety of individual ideas will give vitality to program input. Leadership may then filter new ideas through their experience to produce a workable program which actually originated in the minds of the people. Often church programming is so complicated that no one understands it except those who prepare it. Consequently, no one is motivated or mobilized by such sophisticated programs. When it is a "program of the people," the congregation will participate more wholeheartedly.

33. Begin with Concern

Creative or innovative activity usually starts with a problem to be solved. In the Alliance for Evangelism, "areas of concern" are substituted for the word "problem." The basic areas of concern deal with the program of local evangelism. Sometimes innovative activity becomes a powerfully disruptive force that shatters the *status quo*. Perhaps this is what the church needs! Since the conservative or formal approach to programming has not worked, the church should be willing to try something innovative, or at least think about it.

34. Source of Creative Thinking

An individual is the source of innovative and creative thinking; accordingly, a proper atmosphere to spark clear thinking and a means of recording the ideas is necessary. A committee may develop the individual's ideas and plan a program to implement them, but creativity takes place in the mind of one person. Even though creativity has a popular connotation, and is thought of as a modern wonder drug, it is not all powerful or painless. Creativity produces new thinking and new ways of doing things. The Action Group process helps to make creative and innovative thinking usable in the church. Action Groups are the temporary working units of the Alliance for Evangelism. (See No. 45, 46.)

35. Protection for Creative People

New ways threaten the old ways, and those

who are bound to the old system may prove highly intolerant. This very fact causes many to be reluctant in expressing their creative ideas. Nevertheless, if the church is to bring about innovation, the creative people must be protected. The Action Group approach to general areas of concern in local evangelism meets the need for this creative expression. By participating in an Action Group and having the group itself come to a consensus and recommend various procedures as possible solutions to evangelism problems, the individual thinker does not feel threatened. The new thinking is first filtered through the Action Group, then reported as group work.

36. *Freedom of Expression*

The creative process is not easily structured. Often it is not responsive to any conscious effort to initiate or control it. It becomes a dynamic force that operates spasmodically and never methodically. Therefore, it is important that the Action Group be open-ended and unstructured and each participant be given the freedom to express himself as he feels, sincerely and openly. This is why the Action Groups must meet on several occasions in order to give each participant adequate opportunity to get his creative juices flowing. There is no way to actually make a person more creative. The only thing which can be done is to somehow attempt to create an atmosphere conducive to the release of the potential creativity that is already present. The Action Group filters the ideas, records and summarizes the suggestions and passes them on to others for evaluation and implementation.

37. *Freshness of Perception*

The truly creative person has an openness about

him. He is a keen observer of the action around him. Those who are gifted in the area of creativity normally manage to keep a freshness of perception and an unspoiled awareness of life. One thing learned about creative people is that they often heighten their awareness of some aspects of life by ignoring other aspects. This is another reason why it is necessary to cloister the Action Group and protect it from extraneous thoughts and distracting activities. The creative person is rather independent. Yet, he is often a flexible person who has a capacity to find order in experience.

38. *Obstacles in the Mind*

A climate conducive to creativity and innovative programming cannot be produced unless the church understands those things which prevent such thinking. Most of the obstacles are found in the mind rather than in the physical or material circumstances of the congregation. The difficult problem is to cope with the attitudes and habitual activities that permitted such false concepts of evangelism in the first place.

39. *Plenty of Ideas*

There is usually no real shortage of new ideas. Any churchman knows that many people have criticisms and suggestions, but usually offer them in ways which they are not received. The task then of the Alliance for Evangelism is to structure through the Action Group approach a place where these congregational ideas may receive a hearing. Once they have been heard and recorded, they can then be filtered through the experience of the church leadership and received as input into the future programming of the church.

40. *Shock of Total Program*

Sometimes shock therapy is necessary to shake the congregation into an awareness that change is needed. The defenses of church leadership are usually so stubborn that some kind of complacency shock treatment is the only way to produce any change. The best approach to developing impact on the congregation is for the pastor to make the church aware of the mass of evangelism input from the Action Groups. This should produce an overwhelming reality that change is coming in the outreach ministry. When a whole new program is produced and presented to the congregation, the shock of the total program and conceptual change should cause the church to begin to move in the direction of change and break the hold of inertia.

Church program suffers from inertia: it either stands still or keeps moving in the same direction unless it is drastically affected by some outside force. This is precisely the problem to be solved. The church has not won the world or, for that matter, many of the children and friends of Christians. Why must programs be perpetuated that are not working? If the program is not helping, perhaps it could be discontinued without really hurting. Inertia represents the *status quo* and everyone resists change. Shock in some form is usually necessary to shake people loose from the force of inertia. Patience and adequate motivation can provide the impact to create a desire for change.

41. *Process of Individual Narrowing*

Why is it so hard for churches to change? There is a process called "individual narrowing" which occurs in the lives of most people. As they grow older, they eliminate all the things they do not do well or enjoy doing; consequently, they develop a very narrow view of life and seem satisfied to walk this narrow path. With almost no flexibility, the congregation ends up in a straitjacket of complicated programs and policies which stiffle its very existence.

42. *Choking Underbrush of Programs*

A choking underbrush of left-over programs literally saps the life out of the church. Traditional leaders spend most of their time explaining how they do things and saying, "That won't work here." Consequently, in order to protect territory and leadership, they often appeal to higher moral ground. Somehow rapid growth and change are identified with the secular and godlessness of the age. This is very unfortunate. Change is necessary and will always be produced when growth takes place. Creativity has a tendency to leave some ragged edges. It is necessary even if things are not very tidy.

43. *Problem of "How To"*

Older leaders are preoccupied with "how we do it," yet new and innovative leaders often become bogged down in "how to do it." The "how to" approach causes serious problems because it puts an overemphasis on method, technique and procedure. The goal or objective is often lost in the process of doing the work. Program becomes more important than people. Methods are enthroned. Form seems to triumph over spirit. Although a concern for "how to do it" is necessary and a healthy part of evangelism and church growth, there must be no empty worship of method. Some individuals lose confidence in their personal ability to function without the complicated program "crutches" provided within the standard operating procedures. This can be altered by making significant and necessary improvements in programs and concepts which give individuals more direct involvement in the whole process of outreach programming.

ALLIANCE FOR EVANGELISM

... A team approach to local outreach programming giving the local church a fresh source of New Testament vitality.

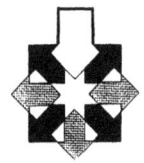

IV
A Task Force for Personal Involvement

The missing link in most church programs is clearly the absence of grass-root participation. Individual church members often feel left out of the decision-making process. Just as a general cannot win a war without the participation and personal contribution of the foot soldier, no pastor can lead an effective New Testament program of evangelism without the personal involvement of his people. This Task Force approach is designed to involve the people. The temporary grouping into working units (Action Groups) has both a problem solving and an operational or behavioral objective. Personal involvement in the evangelism programming process insures more wholehearted participation in the ongoing outreach ministries of the church. Each individual in his own way and in his own words has opportunity to function as a vital part of the whole ministry of the church. When it works, this process can provide the missing link in the chain of evangelism.

44. *A Spirit of Koinonia*

An Alliance for Evangelism may turn an ordinary

church organization into a real Christian fellowship and influence in the community, provided it creates a true spirit of New Testament *koinonia*: sharing, participation, stewardship, communion, fellowship and spiritual involvement. A joint encounter of believers, like radii of a circle, the alliance forms a togetherness with evangelism as its center. This happens because men are willing to commit themselves to Christ and take a stand together for action.

45. *An Opportunity for Lay Participation*

The alliance provides for lay participation in the basic evangelism program of the local church. The goal is to enlist fifty participants in an active outreach and conservation effort. Although provision is made for the use of as few as twenty-one lay persons in the project, a full-strength force is considered to be fifty. The full-strength force is composed of seven Action Groups with seven participants in each with the pastor serving as coordinator. This means a church may use as few as three or as many as seven lay persons in each Action Group.

A very small congregation may function with only twenty-one participants, but each church, regardless of size, should strive for a full-strength force. Small congregations may choose to place some people on more than one group or choose some roving participants who meet with different Action Groups from time to time. Churches forced to use a number smaller than seven must insist on each participant being present for the Action Group sessions. The group dynamics of the project work better with four or more.

Regardless of size, each church should include teens, young marrieds, and older adults in the Action

Group mix. A good age mix in each group is important to the effectiveness of the project, because experience in the group process often stimulates a change to healthier attitudes and relationships. The excitement of youth and the experience of older adults bring a good balance to the work of the Action Group. The small church should use everyone available. Large churches, after a full-strength force has been selected, should include all others in prayer support groups. The purpose is to mobilize the entire church for evangelism.

46. *A Spirit of Cooperation*

Designed to knit the church into a close fellowship, the alliance creates a spirit of cooperation and concern for evangelism in all aspects of church life. Responsibilities of the Action Groups include: (1) finding and cultivating people, (2) doing personal evangelism, (3) increasing church attendance, (4) conserving membership, (5) deepening prayer life, (6) keeping spiritual records, and (7) reenlisting the negligent.

47. *A Task Force Project*

An Alliance for Evangelism is a twelve-month Task Force project divided into two phases: (1) Task Force ONE is a six-month effort primarily concerned with developing leaders and participants and merging them into an innovative force. The basic purpose is to produce creative grass-root solutions to specific areas of concern in local evangelism. (2) Although some ideas and suggestions may be immediately implemented, Task Force TWO is a six-month effort to coordinate and develop the bulk of ideas into workable evangelism programs. The primary emphasis in Task Force TWO is to be implementation.

48. *A Local Problem-Solving Effort*

The need for such an effort grows out of the problem of paternalism, which prevents local problem solving. Some churches are crippled by being directed from the outside. They develop no creative programming. The natural capacity of the congregation is untapped. Often stewardship initiative is choked and no local goals are established by the congregation. Such a resignation to dependents often cripples a local church and handicaps the development of local programming that could solve local problems. In an effort to seek and maintain fellowship, many churches adjust their program and activities. This has many advantages and contributes a great deal to the welfare of new congregations, but there are some limitations.

The sameness of church programming presupposes identical needs and resources everywhere. Rather than gearing a program to local needs, generalizations are necessary that weaken local effectiveness. This often produces a special kind of paternalism that prevents local problem solving and stifles creative initiative. Consequently, church leadership and the congregation as a whole become overly dependent on external assistance. The programs of outreach constantly come *down* in theory to the people rather than *up* from the practical grass-root thinking of the people. The Action Group process stimulates creative thinking by the people.

49. *A Coordinating Council*

Each Action Group of the Alliance for Evangelism consists of a group leader and a group secretary, plus five* additional participants. Each Action Group shall meet at least *twice each month* to discuss plans, projects, and general solutions to assigned and related areas of concern. All Action Group leaders and secretaries shall meet with the pastor once each *month* in a Coordinating Council to report all activities and plans of the various Action Groups. The Coordinating Council provides for follow-up evaluation and encouragement of Action Group activities.

50. *A Six-Month Calendar*

The entire Alliance for Evangelism is to meet four times: once at the beginning, twice during the Action Group process, and at the end for evaluation, planning and inspirational challenge, with the pastor serving as chairman. The pastor may wish to choose

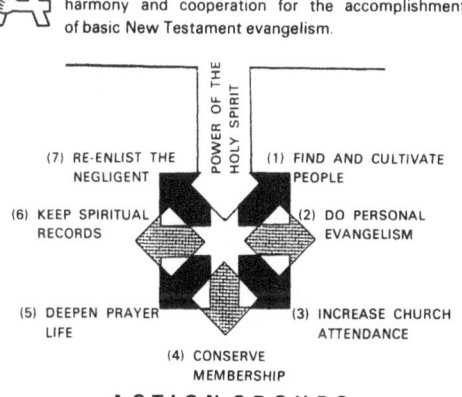

ALLIANCE FOR EVANGELISM
... An "alliance" of believers blended in spiritual harmony and cooperation for the accomplishment of basic New Testament evangelism.

(1) FIND AND CULTIVATE PEOPLE
(2) DO PERSONAL EVANGELISM
(3) INCREASE CHURCH ATTENDANCE
(4) CONSERVE MEMBERSHIP
(5) DEEPEN PRAYER LIFE
(6) KEEP SPIRITUAL RECORDS
(7) RE-ENLIST THE NEGLIGENT

POWER OF THE HOLY SPIRIT

ACTION GROUPS

---

* A very small congregation may use three participants, but each church, regardless of size, is encouraged to use a full-strength force. The very fact of selection may often stimulate more creative involvement.

an associate or a special assistant or secretary to help supervise the Action Groups at work. At the initial meeting of the entire alliance, a six-month calendar of events should be established (see Appendix A) showing all meetings scheduled for the period.

51. *A Back-Up Relationship*

The general responsibilities of each Action Group will overlap at least two other groups. In reality, each Action Group will attack the same basic concerns and potentials of local evangelism from a different vantage point. This overlapping and specific focus must be understood from the beginning. It provides for complimentary back-up relationships between groups. This is a cooperative plan of action and requires the continued understanding and assistance of everyone.

52. *A Guide to Innovative Activity*

Each Action Group shall be given general areas of concern for discussion and creative recommendations. Participants in each Action Group will be furnished an evaluation work sheet and guide to innovative activity (see Appendix B). This work sheet must be completed by each participant for each area of concern individually. This is necessary to be certain each person is thinking for himself. Creativity is an individual matter and is the key to vitality and progress. Action Groups must develop openness, independent thinking, and creative flexibility. Individual participants ought to be concerned with both new ways of doing evangelism and new ways of thinking about evangelism.

53. *A Personal Talk-Sheet*

Once each participant has completed an evaluation work sheet for an area of concern, the Action Group is then ready for an open discussion. The reason for individual advanced work is to provide the participants with a personal talk-sheet. Often it is difficult to do creative thinking while listening to someone else talk. By doing his thinking in advance and putting it on paper, the participant has an agenda from which he may be guided in his own verbal participation within the group.

54. *A Summary Report*

Each Action Group secretary is to observe and creatively listen to the group discussion. Her responsibility is to prepare a summary report of each Action Group meeting. Copies should be given to both the Action Group leader and to the pastor. In addition to the regular things such as time and place of meetings, members present, general areas discussed, the report should show conclusions, specific recommendations and/or suggestions. It is from these Action Reports (see Appendix C) that the pastor and the Coordinating Council should be able to implement certain ideas immediately as well as chart their progress towards gaining long-range solutions to problems of local outreach and evangelism. (See Chapter VIII.)

55. *Action Group Goals*

The Action Groups are given names synonymous with their goals. The seven Action Groups are as follows: Action Group 1—find and cultivate people; Action Group 2—do personal evangelism; Action Group 3—increase personal attendance; Action Group 4—conserve membership; Action Group 5—deepen prayer life; Action Group 6—keep spiritual records; Action Group 7—reenlist the negligent.

56. *An Agenda for Discussion*

General guidelines and areas of concern are listed for each group. These items should form an initial agenda for discussion of ways and means of accomplishing the specific assignment of the group. As the discussion broadens, additional areas of concerns should be added to the agenda by the group. The objective is to bring creative innovation to the local program of evangelism. Renewal and evangelism depends on individuals; therefore, the church must make every effort to open avenues of expression and unclog the areas which stiffle creative innovation. The initial areas of concern for each Action Group are as follows:

ACTION GROUPS
GENERAL AREAS OF CONCERN

56A. *Group One: Find and Cultivate People*

1. Develop a personal *responsibility list* of potential converts and church members.
2. Initiate creative, *positive* programs of visitation to open doors of evangelism and prevent absenteeism.
3. Alert church organizations and individuals of persons on the responsibility list.
4. Maintain a flow of *potential persons* cards.
5. Publicize the church and church related activities to create an open-door atmosphere.

56B. *Group Two: Do Personal Evangelism*

1. Involve all believers in active witnessing. Christians must not only "be" witnesses; they must witness.
2. Enlist and train personal soul winners, using available and approved materials.

3. Provide programs and opportunities for personal soul-winning experience.
4. Lead new converts into church fellowship and discipleship.
5. Establish new members in a growing experience of fellowship and stewardship.
6. Keep the local program of evangelism moving ahead in all aspects of church and community life.

56C. *Group Three: Increase Church Attendance*

1. Help people "belong" to the whole church.
2. See that adequate records are kept and used in a positive manner to prevent absenteeism and bring about faithfulness.
3. Educate congregation as to value of church attendance and the meaning of worship.
4. Make church services more meaningful and attractive.
5. Encourage attendance at all services and activities.
6. Plan for transportation and visitor parking.
7. Establish a "telephone chain" information and follow-up system.

56D. *Group Four: Conserve Membership*

1. Seek to bring about an understanding of the ministry of laymen and the priesthood of believers.
2. Help believers grow in grace and in the Word.
3. Assist members in keeping vows to uphold the church by attendance, prayer, support and service.
4. Encourage individual and family worship.
5. Provide necessary activities and opportunities for spiritual growth.
6. Demonstrate care and concern for individuals.
7. Assist pastor in visitation and spiritual oversight.

56E. *Group Five: Deepen Prayer Life*

1. Enlist and help persons in their daily prayer life.
2. Help families establish family devotions.
3. Create and maintain prayer circles, cells, or groups.
4. Encourage the formation of special purpose prayer efforts.
5. Help make the weekly prayer service vital in spirit, significant in attendance, and worthy in program.
6. Establish an annual prayer vigil as a church experience in continuous prayer chain.

56F. *Group Six: Keep Spiritual Records*

1. Maintain adequate "spiritual" records on local congregation: conversion, baptism, membership, stewardship, etc.
2. Consider designing a "spiritual record" card for local use.
3. Correct and complete records which contain spiritual experience, stewardship, and Christian commitment.
4. Furnish vital information to proper personnel for follow-up and counseling.
5. Help make individuals conscious of spiritual progress.

56G. *Group Seven: Reenlist the Negligent*

1. Discover the negligent.
2. Create files for action.
3. Follow up nonresidents by mail or phone.
4. Visit to demonstrate spiritual concern for each individual.
5. Reclaim the inactives for the church.

6. Attempt to determine causes for inactives and program to correct these causes.

57. *A Multiplicity of Ideas*

Action Groups will be expected to produce multiplicity of ideas with a general application to the problem of local evangelism. Ideas derived from the action approach process should be easily classified in two general groups: (1) *Short-run ideas* that are in the area of thoughts, examples, or rule-of-thumb suggestions to guide in the improving of existing programs. (2) *Long-run ideas* of a more conclusive nature that help build new and workable programs and enable more direct participation of the congregation in the outreach ministries of the church.

See Appendix F ("Leader's Sequence Orientation") for a thirty step guide to initiating and completing an Alliance for Evangelism.

ACTION GROUP LEADERS

ALLIANCE FOR EVANGELISM

... A unique project to produce new ways of thinking about and new ways of doing evangelism.

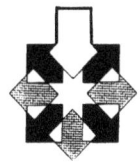

V
A Search for Innovative Ideas

Leadership is vital in the creative search for innovative solutions to local evangelism. The church in general and the work of evangelism in particular have suffered from the lack of lay leadership. A leader sets the pace and has the ingredient of personality which causes others to follow. The successful resolution of problems is an essential quality for leadership. If there were no problems, there would be no need of leaders.

The basic problem to be solved is clear: souls for whom Christ died remain lost. The church, as presently constituted and programmed, has not kept pace with population growth, to say nothing of reaching the whole world for Christ. Something must be done to solve this basic problem. Leaders are needed to set the pace and mold individual Christians into a workable outreach team. Men of dedication, innovative thinking, and spiritual power are needed. God has such men. These men must be found, prepared, and challenged to lead an Alliance for Evangelism.

58. *Selecting Action Group Leaders*

The kind of men selected to lead the Action Group

process is most important. They hold the key to the success of the whole "alliance." Each church must use the men available. After prayer choose the most capable leaders. The Holy Spirit will make them equal to the task. Remember this is a spiritual work. Use the following criteria in selecting Action Group leaders:

    1. Familiarity with church purpose, programs, and procedures.
    2. Strong identification with evangelism.
    3. Successful performance in career, showing capacity to relate to and understand others.
    4. Acceptance by the local congregation as a spiritual man.
    5. Previous group experience is helpful.

59. *Preparing Action Group Leaders*

An Action Group leader may well stand or fall on his skill in working with the group. Leadership skills can be developed. Certain techniques mark the successful leader and contribute to the value of group work and experience. Regardless of previous experience, any leader can improve by working hard enough.

Preparation for serving as an Action Group leader is best accomplished by participating as a member in such a group. The first thing to do, then, is to select the seven potential Action Group leaders and initiate a training encounter. Based on experience as a participant in the activity, the Action Group leader gains confidence for his leadership role in the Alliance for Evangelism.

60. *Three Sessions of Training*

It will be necessary for the pastor to stage at least three Action Group leader training sessions.

Session one should be a free discussion to enable the Action Group leader-trainees to gain an understanding and acceptance of themselves and others. Session two should be a brief orientation to the Alliance for Evangelism project. Session three should be a sample Action Group session with the pastor serving as the Action Group leader and the trainees serving as participants. Select an area of concern (See 56A, no. 1, p. 60). Use the evaluation work sheet and do a summary report.

61. *Background of Discussion Experience*

Theoretically, the public school system and the community should give all Americans an opportunity to "speak one's mind," and thus provide a rich background of group discussion experience. In actuality, many lack this experience. They have not participated as members of planning or free discussion groups. Volunteer agencies in the community find that a small percentage of community population do all the work. The same is true in the church. The Action Group can help change this.

62. *Groups Encourage Creativity*

The group climate encourages creative discussion and stimulates new ideas. When a new perspective of oneself is gained, important insights may result. Fresh viewpoints, greater tolerance of others, and improved communicative and social skills are available for those who wish to grow. Personal growth is possible for participants of any age or maturity level. Include teens, young marrieds, and older adults in the Action Group mix. Experience in the group process can stimulate a change to healthier attitudes and relationships. A good age mix in each Action Group is important.

63. *Excellent Background Experience*

Experience in open discussion, either for group planning or for exchange of view points, is lacking in the educational process and in the adult lives of the majority of people. Participation in group action (discussion) for the sake of learning more about one's own attitude about evangelism is excellent background experience for participation (involvement) in the ongoing programs of evangelism. As each Action Group leader better understands his own thinking about evangelism, he can better stimulate others to participate in outreach ministry.

64. *Adequate Meeting Place*

Action Group meetings should be scheduled for an appropriate room in the church complex. The room should be equipped with comfortable chairs and a place to write. It must be free from the telephone and other distractions. An atmosphere of privacy is essential to the function of the group. The room should be reserved and should be in readiness before the participants arrive. If the meeting must take place outside the church, the place must be appropriate and convenient to the participants. Do not permit the meeting to become a social function. It is not an eating meeting. It is an A-C-T-I-O-N meeting.

65. *Feeling of Togetherness Needed*

The group must be seated properly. More participation will be forthcoming if each member can see all the others. This somehow promotes a feeling of togetherness and causes each one to feel a part of the group. It also eliminates dominating personalities from choosing a key position and from the vantage point dominating the session. Each individual should have a place to write, such as a desk or table.

66. *Clear Objectives Necessary*

Action Group leaders must understand that the Alliance for Evangelism defines "problems" as "areas of concern." There must be an objective, a clear indication where you want to go. Problems are simply those barriers that must be moved to obtain objectives. Solutions cannot be found until the problem has been clearly defined. An objective is necessary in understanding the barriers that must be removed. Evaluate the areas of concern assigned. What additions to the agenda can be made within the overall responsibility of the specific Action Group? Add them! (See 56A-G, pp. 60-63.)

67. *Participant Part of the Problem*

Everyone is both part of the problem and part of the solution. As he understands his own personal difficulties and lack of participation in the ongoing program of evangelism, he will begin to see a partial solution to the problem. As he makes his own personal dedication and is convinced that he must personally participate in the daily ministry of soul winning, an overall solution begins to emerge.

68. *Many Possible Solutions*

There is a difference between a problem and a question. There is but one right answer to a question; however, there are many possible solutions to a problem. There may be no right or wrong solution to a problem. The order of preference of the solutions depends on a great many factors. It is the external factors that determine the rank order of the possible solutions. These are sometimes called the "specifications" of the problem. A workable solution cannot be found as long as people talk about different things. It is necessary, then, for specific guidelines for the discussion to be made clear. Each participant must understand the area of concern and discuss one particular aspect of the problem at a time.

69. *Opinions Usually Differ*

Objectives and problems are facts that can be agreed upon when mutually understood. Solutions or opinions usually differ until a compromise has been effected. Objectives and problems are accepted because there is no specific action inherent in them. The presentation of a proposed solution to a problem is the signal for the raising of objections. If the proposed solution requires change, it will be automatically attacked. Often the very best solutions are killed before they have been seriously considered. Courage to try the new, untested, even novel solution must be encouraged. It is well to remember that Christ himself rode into Jerusalem on a donkey on which a man had never sat.

70. *Unprejudicial Search for Solutions*

There are no simple solutions to a complex problem. There must be a total solution if the total problem is to be solved. No source of ideas, or methods of procuring them, should be overlooked in the unprejudicial search for workable solutions. Any solution to a problem is one method of removing the problem as an obstacle to progress toward an objective.

71. *Elicit Creative Ideas*

The Action Group has a very narrow purpose.

The objective is to elicit as many creative ideas from the participants as can be applied to the specific area of concern assigned to the group. The Action Group leader must be careful not to permit the discussion to stray into areas which are not his responsibility. Focus is important. Zero in on specific areas and dig for additional suggestions.

72. Accept Rather Than Reject Ideas

The Action Group leader must take the necessary steps to insure total participation in the group. A catalyst himself, the leader must act in ways to keep the stream of ideas flowing. As he takes in ideas, clarifies them and shares them again with the entire group, everyone can get into the creative act. An Action Group leader must accept rather than reject ideas. Even if he disagrees with what is said, the leader must not stiffle participation by asserting his negative response. Acceptance of a suggestion or idea in the Action Group process does not necessarily mean agreement with it, but it does mean giving everyone an even chance to participate. The leader should not pass judgment on ideas, but accept and enlarge upon them.

73. Reflect Participant's View

The Action Group leader is responsible for reflecting various points of view given by the participants. If the participant's statement or view is not clear, it would be the responsibility of the leader to ask a key or probing question to attempt a reflection of the participant's view. This takes concentration and practice. The advantages are obvious. Such a method encourages the input of original ideas in an understandable way.

74. *Clarify and Rephrase Statements*

Occasionally, participants will make statements that are out of focus. When the point is not clear, the leader should polish these nuggets into brilliant ideas by clarifying and rephrasing them. When a statement is clarified, it should also be made relevant to the area of concern or issue at hand. Oftentimes a small idea that is closely related to the larger picture can be restated and focused so that the group can consider it in a broader view.

75. *Use Hitchhiking*

A basic purpose of the Action Group process is to obtain as many ideas as possible. The number of ideas are almost inexhaustible when a good leader does his job. The purpose, of course, is to get excellent thinking out into the open. When someone comes up with a bright idea, rather than considering it as a closed issue, the leader should ask for additional points of view or related ideas. This is known as "hitchhiking," since one person takes an expressed idea and mentally travels with it, adding his own thinking to it.

76. *Silence Sparks Creativity*

The Action Group leader must not be afraid of silence. Creativity comes in spurts. Sometimes there will be a few moments when no one has anything to say. Instruct the group that when these occasions come they should not be impatient, but to use these quiet mements for reflection and prayerful consideration of the issue at hand. Do not let a silent pause become awkward. It gives the group time to think. This is the reason they are assembled in the first place. Give the process a chance to work. Do not rush group action. Creativity cannot be forced!

77. *Learn by Listening*

Some participants will talk too much and some will not talk enough. Others will say things off the subject. Still others may say very little, but what they do say will be worth the group's time. Encourage everyone to listen creatively.

The key to working with an Action Group is to stay in a positive and pleasant mood. A leader's personality must show both confidence and friendliness. The leader must demonstrate his desire to be of service. Cooperation and participation will come to all group leaders who pray, plan, and patiently work with the group process.

78. *Levels of Mental Activity*

Activating the thinking process is not an easy task. Action Group leaders must understand that participants actually listen on three levels of mental activity: (1) Level of nonhearing. The participant appears to listen. He looks at the speaker and even nods periodically or utters deceptive indicators of attention, but his mind is closed. (2) Level of hearing. He hears words being said, but they do not register. He does not absorb the facts. He may be able to repeat words or phrases spoken, but the ideas evaporate. (3) Level of thinking. The listener thinks about what is said and does mental work. The process includes evaluating what is said, comparing it with something else, analyzing for its causes, predicting likely outcomes, or making a decision about it. Participants must listen at the level of thinking to function as a vital part of the Action Group.

79. *Springboards to Discussion*

Action Group leaders should develop various techniques to be used as springboards to discussion. There are several ways this can be done:

1. An informational talk can be given at the beginning of the session. It would assist the conversation if a typed reference sheet were passed to the participants.
2. A check list or rating sheet may be used in comparing various things.
3. The role-playing approach can be used.
4. A provocative subject in which group members are emotionally involved often needs no introduction or springboard. However, the Action Group leader should steer the direction of the discussion by the phrasing of a lead-off question.
5. Occasionally, one whole session may be used as preparation for the next major discussion in a following session.
6. An effective springboard device consists of enlarging upon a subject of interest learned in casual conversation before the formal opening of the session. This may be used to help shy members forget their self-consciousness and really "talk" in the discussion.
7. Occasionally, a leader may see a need for a completely free talk-feast and should encourage frank and open expression. No springboard is needed for such a truly nondirected session.

80. *A Method of Stimulating Discussion*

Brainstorming is an effective method of stimulating discussion and securing agenda ideas for later meetings. Here is how it operates. The participants are seated in the regular Action Group session. The general problem or specific area of concern is stated. They are then asked to think about the difficulty.

In an atmosphere of "anything goes," the participants throw out whatever comes into their heads. The theory is that some good ideas and even some outlandish ones will trigger other good ideas. A secretary transcribes the proceedings and later the ideas are examined and filtered through the leadership. Some of the ideas can go directly on the Action Report; others may form items on the agenda and additional areas of concern for regular Action Group sessons.

Criticism of any idea is flatly barred as long as the sessions are in progress. Negative or killer phrases are barred. Comments such as "that won't work" or "it's been done before" are blocked by the Action Group leader. This is sometimes done by ringing a bell or blowing a whistle to stimulate laughter and relax the tension so the group can get back into a freewheeling mood. Some of the ideas will wind up in the wastebasket, but many of them are worth developing. Sometimes even more important than the ideas is the stimulation the experience gives the participants in using imagination instead of old-line chatter.

81. *Action Group Resource*

The following basic concerns should be considered as Action Group resource stimulators in five areas: program, personnel, organization, fellowship, and renewal. These preview paragraphs from *Why Churches Die* are designed to stimulate new ways of thinking about, and new ways of doing, evangelism.

82. *Program-Centered Concerns*

Many problems of the church are program centered. Basically, Christianity has lost its Sunday punch because the first day of the week has become the psychological last day. Consequently, it no longer sets the pace and pattern for the activities of the week. This precipitates a theology of coercion that causes the clergy to spend most of their time attempting to challenge and motivate constituency involvement in the Great Commission. This theology of coercion breeds a methodology designed to reach men and almost negates the power of personal Christian experience. Complicated methods and overprogramming limits the mobilization of the congregation because the constituency does not understand. When programs fail, often the people are blamed. Thus, the church becomes imprisoned by previous patterns and perpetuates programs that are ineffective. Perhaps the greatest problem of all is that the church building complex, which should be the force with which to work, becomes the field of operation. Consequently, in the hustle to keep the organization alive, clergy and congregants are often unaware that the organism is dying.

83. *Personnel-Centered Concerns*

Personnel-centered concerns begin with the pulpit and the downgrading of proclamation. This causes the purpose of the church as the living body of Christ to be thwarted. Consequently, a gap grows between the pulpit and pew, producing weak links that endanger the chain of evangelism. Perhaps the most serious consequence of the weak pulpit is the preaching of cheap grace. This produces poor converts and causes the church to reach converts who have an intellectual apprehension of truth but often possess little knowledge. Thus, the church has difficulty in leading the convert into an active life as a Christian disciple. When converts do not grow in grace and knowledge, it is impossible to produce believers who can be entrusted with the saving witness as "apostles of the streets."

84. *Organization-Centered Concerns*

Churchmen often consider doctrinal orthodoxy sufficient to guarantee growth and progress for the church. This attitude obstructs the inherent factors of growth and causes churchmen to be content with mediocrity. The willingness to settle for something less than the best causes the church to suffer from spiritual disease and to become strangulated in vital areas of growth and progress. The willingness to settle for mediocre operations also brings about a lack of global perspective and produces a neglect of planting new churches.

85. *Fellowship-Centered Concerns*

As the church concentrates on a narrow definition of fellowship, a "no-harvest" theology grows. Many activities have no soul-winning objective. The church seems to concentrate on keeping the constituency happy. This precipitates a "come" strategy where the church opens the doors and waits for the people. Since fellowship is not strong enough to hold any group together, an active constituency drift exists, which is usually concealed by statistics. In an effort to seek and maintain fellowship with a denomination, conference or material supply source, churches adjust their program and activities to maintain a connection with a parent group. This produces a paternalism that often prevents local problem solving and causes an overdependency on external assistance. The problems of fellowship also wall-in converts and isolate them from their potential. It also causes the church constituency to place priority on secondary projects and often is responsible for individuals being lost in the crowd.

86. *Renewal-Centered Concerns*

Somehow in the whole scheme of renewal, the dynamic structure of the church is disregarded and the automatic nature of revival is frustrated. A basic problem is the neglect of the priesthood of believers which causes a "passive sheep" structure to prevail within the church and generally leads to the church taking a wrong route to renewal. The courage to prune personnel and programs and to administer the cure for spiritual disease is almost nonexistent. Both clergy and laity seem to be preoccupied with program, personnel, organization or fellowship at the expense of renewal. Consequently, men unintentionally hinder the process of renewal in the life of the church.

It would be helpful if each Action Group leader and the church staff could read the entire text of *Why Churches Die* by Hollis L. Green (Bethany Fellowship, Inc., Minneapolis, Minnesota 55438; available in paperback).

ALLIANCE FOR EVANGELISM

...A concept of concern that translates the language of words about evangelism into a language of relationships that reaches people for Christ.

ACTION GROUP
PARTICIPANTS

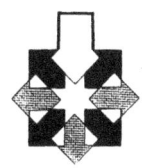

VI

A Forum for Lay Expression

Creative people want to feel useful. They search for meaningful expression of their personal ideas. Some haunting dissatisfaction usually motivates their work. The creative process is as individualistic as the persons doing the creating. Yet, sometime or other all creative people must go through essentially the same steps: find sources of inspiration, express their ideas, evaluate their expression, and refine the finished product into an acceptable form.

The Action Group process will assist in the expression of individual ideas. Nothing worthwhile comes without difficulty. Preparing for creative activity can be difficult, but preparation must be made. Each individual must see his worth as a person. Personal prayer, reading of the Scriptures, and a genuine desire to be led by the Holy Spirit are basic to effective participation in *spiritual* work. Although it may not seem so, participation in an Action Group to find creative solutions to the problems which plague evangelism is a spiritual task which requires dedicated disciples of Christ.

87. *Participation in an Action Group*

Participation in an Action Group is a natural extension of everyday life. A great deal of living is actually functioning in what sociologists call primary groups, that is, groups which consist of people in face-to-face relationships. Many also have experience in experimental groups working together to solve problems or engage in specific tasks.

Although creativity is usually the work of individuals, current research suggests that groups working together usually do a better job of solving problems and making judgments. This is caused by a combination of things. The presence of others stimulates the thinking process. Two heads are better than one, because they both complement and criticize. The presence of possible critics causes one to focus his thinking and be challenged to make useful input. Interaction is a key factor in the group process. Each one is prompted by the attitude and action of the group.

88. *Problem of Unused Abilities*

No one has achieved his full potential. Everyone has latent abilities, hidden talents, and undeveloped capacities. This is a universal problem. The church is not exempt. The church is filled with individuals who are not participating fully in life or in the church. Since a good way to expose hidden talents is to get people involved in a growing process of concern about themselves and others, the Alliance for Evangelism is structured around the Action Group approach.

89. *A Secret of Happiness*

A secret of happiness is being useful. Participating in an Action Group is meaningful involvement and

will help an individual develop his potential, thus becoming:
1. More efficient
2. Free from internal and external barriers to creative achievements
3. Free from prejudice in thinking
4. Able to suggest various solutions to problems
5. Independent and versatile in thinking
6. Able to get along with people under pressure
7. Better able to use intuitive powers
8. Able to produce unlimited ideas

90. *A Sequence of Events*

There is a sequence of events which occurs over and over wherever successful people are found. Individuals of achievement seem to: (1) become sensitive to a life purpose, (2) establish basic objectives, (3) determine the problems needing to be solved, (4) find solutions to the problems, and (5) evaluate results of applying the solutions. A direct application can be made of these five steps to an effective program of evangelism. The first is obvious. When purpose is established, the others seem to follow logically. Each person must have purpose in life to cope with the struggle and rise to true achievement. Participation requires personal commitment (see Appendix D). Only with purpose and commitment can priorities be established and personal creative power be put to work. Winning people to Christ is a noble and motivating purpose. That is what involvement in an Action Group is all about.

91. *Achievement of Maximum Usefulness*

Asked about his success record in solving different problems, a man of achievement explained his personal philosophy this way: "If it *ought* to be done, it *can* be done. If it *can* be done, *I can do it.*" Self-confidence in problem solving generates great creative power. Paul said, "I can do all things through Christ...." His success in evangelism is well documented in the New Testament. Self-confidence comes from accepting what God says about believers and realizing that the power of the Holy Spirit is present to enable and equip for the task. After the difficult Council at Jerusalem, James wrote, "It seemed good to the Holy Spirit, and to us." The achievement of maximum usefulness comes as one seeks to fulfill God's noble purpose for his life. As a Christian, each person has a part in God's eternal program.

92. *Achievement Begins with Dissatisfaction*

Self-starting begins with a problem to be solved. In crisis, man is provided with both opportunity and challenge. If necessity is the mother of invention, then problem finding is the cornerstone of creative thinking. Almost anyone can come up with workable ideas if he will simply identify a problem and think clearly about solutions. Many great achievements began with dissatisfaction with ineffective ways of doing things. The tiresome, unsanitary task of slicing pieces of cheese for each customer led J. L. Kraft to the idea of prepackaged cheese. Rotting pineapples in Hawaii caused Mr. Dole to think of selling pineapple juice in cans. Mr. Gerber, tired of mashing peas for his baby, did something about it. So also in evangelism, simply look for things that are not working in the local program of evangelism. What can be done about them? How can it be done better? Seek a simple answer. Good! You are on your way to involvement in an action process that could change your attitudes about evangelism and turn ineffective methods of evangelism into personalized action.

93. An Amazing Part of Idea Gathering

The amazing part of idea gathering is that many of the best ones seemingly pop into your head without effort. Inspiration happens at unexpected times—while shaving, cooking breakfast, driving or walking in the park. This is not some kind of magic; it is the subconscious taking over. Thinking about the problem and the attempts to find simple solutions got the miraculous subconscious working on the answer. Become concerned and the mental resources go to work. Put yourself to the test—pray, think, read, submit to the Holy Spirit. You can be a productive member of the Action Group group process.

94. Available Solutions for Evangelism

Creativity is infinite in scope and finds expression over the entire range of life. Benjamin Franklin once said, "To cease to think creatively is to cease to live." Early American settlers were self-sufficient. Church pioneers were effective with inadequate resources. Solutions were available then, and solutions are available today. Christians must open their eyes and see the great potential for evangelism. Participation and concern for the ongoing process of outreach ministry seems to be the key. Solutions *can* be found.

95. A Forum of Expression

The Action Group is a forum for the expression of personal ideas. Ideas are often awkward little things and difficult to express. They do not work unless the originator does. Once an idea has been conceived it must be expressed in understandable terms. Creative solutions are needed. These precious ideas will come from people—people just like you. You have something to say. Say it! The idea must be brought to life by expressing it in words and getting others to actually listen to what you are saying. To get your ideas accepted you must overcome inertia in others, promote change by implementing your decisions and expressing your desires. All this must be done in cooperation with other members of the Action Group.

96. *A Spoke in the Wheel*

A wise old pioneer was asked which spoke in his wagon wheel was the most important. He replied, "They are all important. I would not have a wheel if I had only one spoke." Obviously, no single person is as good as the Action Group altogether. It is likewise true that each person as a spoke in a wheel is of great value. Each filling his place, bearing his part of the load can make everything move forward smoothly. You may not consider yourself an effective communicator because you cannot command attention when you speak. If you feel your most exciting suggestions frequently fall flat when you attempt to verbalize them, the Action Group process will help you. In the Action Group your ideas are as good as anyone else's. You are a spoke in the wheel. People will act on your ideas. Of course you can help by making the group want to listen. This can be done by presenting your ideas in clear and simple terms. In this way you can effectively sell your thinking to the group.

97. *Speak with Confidence*

The group is already interested in the subject.

Each one is thinking about solutions. They want to hear what you have to say, but you must say it with enthusiasm and authority. Otherwise they may hear —glassy-eyed—but not actually listen to a single word. Speak clearly and confidently. Your ideas are as good as theirs. Show your sincerity. Think the idea through, then be confident and speak with assurance. It helps to record the idea before you speak. If an idea can be put in writing, it can be communicated.

98. *Listen to Others*

Action Group participants must also listen to others. This is a vital part of the process. It helps to stimulate thinking as well as to give the other fellow a sounding board. Do not sell other people short. Use their thinking. Participate. Hitchhike on their thoughts. Hearing and listening are not the same thing. Hearing is purely a physical experience. Listening is both physical and mental. A person cannot help but hear the sound of the words; however, getting the message is another thing altogether.

99. *A Process of Understanding*

Listening is a process of understanding and acting upon what is heard. The act may not be more than evaluating what is heard or changing the mind or making a decision, but when you truly listen, you must do something. When you hear, you neither think nor act. When you listen, you put facts together, judge the situation and act. Listening is a process of focusing on what is actually said and meant. Listening is not remembering; it is understanding. Understanding is the ability to see relationships between different facts and to grasp the fundamental ideas behind them. Listening is the other half of talking.

The brain is a supersonic computer. It can imagine, judge, decide, review; it can actually view 10,000 remembered facts and in a flash bring up the only one that matters at the moment. It can file sensations and impressions for instant future reference. And it never stops working. Let it work. Let it work for evangelism.

100. *Stick to the Point*

Put your thinking cap on when the Action Group is in session. Attempt to hold the attention of the group when you speak. Speak up to be heard and speak clearly to be understood. More time must not be taken than the subject is worth. Stick to the point and keep your speech short. Excessive time often unwittingly produces repetition; thus you say things already obvious to the group. This does not keep the group active because the pace of new information is too slow. Be conscious of the pace and bring in fresh information to keep the mind alert. When repeating what another has said, you must always give additional information. Concrete words should be used to keep the group visualizing thoughts. Practical application of these things in your regular conversation will improve your contribution in the Action Group session.

101. *Concentration on the Moment*

Participants must try to practice spontaneity in the Action Group sessions. Spontaneity means "full response, adequately given in the situation." It implies complete concentration on the moment and the best possible reaction—one person to another—in that moment. Spontaneity takes into consideration individual differences, that one person might react by disagreeing with the speaker; another person might give enthusiastic support; a third responder may sit quietly, thinking over what is said.

102. Self-interest Limits Contribution

Spontaneity is possible when a participant is not inhibited and constricted by his own self-interest. When he is so self-conscious that he habitually reacts in terms of himself, he cannot engage in spontaneous interaction with others. Consequently, his contribution to the Action Group session is limited.

103. Attitudes of Participants

In preparing for participation in an Action Group of the Alliance for Evangelism, a participant should try to take the following attitudes:

1. I want help with personal effectiveness in evangelism and I am ready to learn from others. Their opinions and viewpoints will give a perspective which I alone do not have.

2. I will try to do for others in my Action Group what I want them to do for me. I will guard against self-centered thinking and will try to put myself in the place of others when they are speaking.

3. I will try to be frank and honest—not to put up a front. If I feel bitter or irritated, I will say so and explain the reasons. If I am asked for a frank opinion, I will give it. Since everyone in the group is trying to understand himself and others, as a soul winner it is important to relax and be oneself.

4. I will try to be sensitive to the way other group participants feel. When support or reassurance is needed by someone, I will try to give it in all sincerity.

5. If a discussion or individual's action upsets me,

I will see the Action Group leader about this. Also, I will discuss personal things with him which may have a bearing on the specific task of the group.

104. *Evaluation of Participation*

An individual member of an Action Group may analyze his personal participation pattern in discussion through the following questions:

1. Do I usually sit back and listen to a discussion, giving everyone opportunity to participate, or do I tend to talk too much?
2. Do I usually think my ideas are superior to those of others, and close my mind to an opposite point of view?
3. Do I tend to make snap judgments of people: generalize from a particular instance; use guilt by association?
4. Do I feel a responsibility for filling in silence or for steering the discussion? Does it bother me when the group wanders away from the point of the discussion?
5. What are my personal biases? Can I be objective in controversial areas?
6. Are there some topics on which I "clam up"? —for instance, personal devotional time, time spent in prayer, number of individuals led to Christ in the past year? Why do I have these painful or tender areas? Should I ask the Action Group leader for advice concerning my participation in such discussions?
7. Do I willingly admit my personal shortcomings? My failure to participate totally in the ongoing program of daily evangelism?

105. *Implementation of Ideas*

Although ultimate implementation is left to the Coordinating Council, Task Force TWO and the church staff, many aspects of the idea-gathering phase could be implemented immediately. Some suggestions may be placed into operation through minor changes in present programs. Others will automatically become an almost unnoticed part of the concepts and thinking of the congregation. The most important aspect of immediate implementation is the changes the individual participants of each Action Group makes in his personal life.

All the effort to bring creative solutions to the program of evangelism will fail unless the participants are changed in the process. As a concept becomes clear, put it into operation in your daily life. If an idea is practical and workable, implement it in your part of the church program. Put the ideas, thoughts, suggestions about evangelism to work. Sure, the church program will eventually be changed to reflect the new way of thinking and new ways of doing evangelism, but changes must be made now —changes in your life, changes in your attitudes, changes in your daily involvement in outreach ministry. Take courage. As the Spirit leads, make these personal changes. Get involved in soul winning. You can change the church by changing those things under your control. Get changed. Get together. Get going. Souls are lost. You can find them and lead them to a saving knowledge of Christ and into the fellowship of His church.

ALLIANCE FOR EVANGELISM

...A new zest for spiritual life gained through involving laymen in an active program of outreach ministry.

ACTION GROUP SECRETARIES

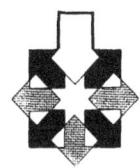

VII
A Process of Summary Reporting

The idea-gathering process is not an end in itself. Although the very act of participation sets in motion certain beneficial attitudes, the full value cannot be realized without evaluation and application of the ideas. The search for creative expression is almost fruitless without a plan for harvesting the discussion seed thoughts. This is why the secretary is so vital to the Action Group approach. The note-taking, the recording of suggested solutions, the summary of innovative ideas, and the Action Report of recommendations are all essential to the complete process. Choose and prepare the Action Group secretaries carefully. Each one has a most important function.

106. *Choosing Action Group Secretaries*

There has never been an oversupply of good secretaries, but each congregation usually has several "working" secretaries. Also, there are experienced secretaries who no longer work. From among the working and the experienced, choose seven Action Group secretaries. Included in the hoped-for abilities and qualities of a good secretary is excellence in the mechanical skills: note-taking and typing. Should a secretary be selected who has lost her speed, a tape recorder can be a great help. Closely related to the mechanical skills is the need for being good at detail. The ability to summarize is important. Choose the best talent available for the task.

107. *An Orientation Session for Secretaries*

The pastor should structure at least one orientation session with the Action Group secretaries. All aspects of their role in the Action Group process should be covered. The Action Report is vital to the effectiveness of the Alliance for Evangelism. The importance of adequate note-taking, summary reports, and follow-up should be stressed.

108. *A Most Important Role*

A few minutes well spent can save needless hours. Minutes—the record kind—reported accurately will preserve the creative expression and capture for useful evaluation the thinking of the group. The Action Group secretary has a most important role in the Action Group process.

109. *Conscientious and Efficient Function*

Success of the Action Group process depends a great deal on the conscientious and efficient function of the secretary. Her role includes efficient preparation and planning beforehand, concise and clear reporting during the session, and prompt, effective follow-through when the meeting is over. Many of the "man-hours" spent will be wasted unless the meeting is adequately summarized and conclusions and recommendations are passed on to the proper authorities for implementation. The Action Report should be carefully prepared immediately following each meeting.

110. *Meeting Arrangements*

The Action Group secretary should be certain that the Action Group sessions are scheduled on the church calendar and that each participant knows the time and place. A friendly reminder by mail or phone will help attendance. Reserve a meeting room well in advance of each session. Select a room of adequate size but not too large. Small groups are overpowered by large rooms; consequently, interchange will suffer. Check on the seating arrangement before meeting time. Be sure there are enough chairs, places to write, and paper and pencils for use of the group. Prepare all necessary materials, forms, etc. Keep the room cool. Give it a good ventilating before the session and see that the temperature stays a little on the cool side. If you plan refreshments, do so for a middle of the session break or at closing time. Do not permit the Action Group session to become a social event. It is a work session.

111. *Members of the Same Team*

Be gracious. Be dependable. Be a good member of the team. Take an enthusiastic interest in the ideas and suggestions of the group. Be certain that your energies, time, and thoughts are at the disposal of others. Follow instructions and see that tasks for which you are responsible get done. Tact and judgment are important. These traits help you to know when to talk and when to remain silent and do your "note-taking." Remain calm and controlled. Do not exhibit any impatience with the pace of the group process. Everyone is on the same team.

112. Note-Taking and Summary Reports

Remember, you have an Action Report to complete immediately following the session, copies of which are to be given to the pastor and the Action Group leader for use in the Coordinating Council. Take ample notes. Too many notes are better than too few. Record as much of the conversation as you can. Use a tape recorder if your shorthand or speedwriting is too slow.

Attempt to take important statements verbatim, but *do not* identify the speaker. This is a special procedure for Action Groups. All that is reported out must be identified as the work of the group process. Everyone receives equal credit for the creative work of the group. Although one may speak the actual words, the action, the participation and the group thinking help to spark the creative expression. Always verify facts, statements, summaries, or recommendations with the Action Group leader before filing the Action Report (Appendix C). Completed Evaluation Work Sheets (Appendix B) should be collected and turned in with the Action Report to the pastor. These will be needed later by Task Force TWO.

The Action Report is a summary report completed immediately following each session while all the discussion is fresh. It must be done without delay. Present briefly a concise statement of main points coming out of the discussion. Some statements should be reported verbatim, others summarized. Report clearly the conclusions or recommendations of the group. Use the backside of the Action Report to record a list of ideas, thoughts, or suggestions expressed by the group. This is very important. The success of the whole program of implementation depends on an adequate and accurate record of the Action Group process. The secretaries' work is a most vital part of the Alliance for Evangelism.

 **TASK FORCE TWO**

ALLIANCE FOR EVANGELISM

... An effective lay participation effort to knit the church into a closer fellowship and mobilize the congregation through better dissemination of evangelism plans and projects.

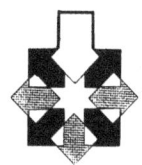

VIII

An Implementation of Local Solutions

The Action Group process is not complete until the creative thinking and innovative solutions are applied directly to the life and program of the church. This implementation process begins with the work of the Coordinating Council who regularly evaluate the Action Reports and encourage group work. Once the idea-gathering phase is complete and all the suggestions are reported, the major aspect of implementation begins. Task Force TWO is charged with finishing the project.

Task Force TWO is not just a supplement to the Action Group approach; it is the completion of it. It is the finishing act to give practical application and to ensure the actual fulfillment of the Alliance for Evangelism. The reports, the evaluation work sheets and other materials gathered by Task Force ONE furnish an answer or the means of answering the problems of local evangelism. A practical application must be worked out and recommended to the church leaders. This process should free the leadership to carry out the practical suggestions of the people in the official programs of the local church. Implementation of Action Group ideas in every aspect of church life and ministry is the goal of the Alliance for Evangelism.

113. *Personnel for Task Force TWO*

The Coordinating Council *plus one* member from each Action Group become the personnel for Task Force TWO. Although some ideas and suggestions will be immediately implemented by Action Group participants working within the existing structure of the church, Task Force TWO is a six-month effort to coordinate and develop the bulk of ideas into workable local evangelism programs. The primary emphasis here is the implementation of the long-run ideas. The church cannot wait until Sunday. A seven-day program of outreach is needed. Evangelism must become the life-style of all believers.

114. *Procedure of Classifying*

The procedure is to sort and classify the ideas, suggestions, recommendations, thoughts, concerns and burdens expressed on the evaluation work sheets (Appendix B) and the Action Reports (Appendix C). The sorting and classification should follow the seven areas of the Action Group structure. Once the classification is completed, a report should be prepared in each of the seven areas: (1) finding and cultivating people, (2) doing personal evangelism, (3) increasing church attendance, (4) conserving membership, (5) deepening prayer life, (6) keeping spiritual records, and (7) reenlisting the negligent.

115. *Report in Three Parts*

Each report should be in three parts: first a report on improvements, projects, programs, or changes already implemented in the area; second, a complete listing of all ideas and suggestions, as yet unused in each category; third, specific recommendations and suggestions as to their practical use. The complete report on Action Group One "Find and Cultivate People" would be listed under the title "*Plus One*: Finding and Cultivating People." Others would follow the same procedure, "*Plus Two*: Doing Personal Evangelism," etc. as follows:

Plus One: Finding and Cultivating People
Plus Two: Doing Personal Evangelism
Plus Three: Increasing Church Attendance
Plus Four: Conserving Membership
Plus Five: Deepening Prayer Life
Plus Six: Keeping Spiritual Records
Plus Seven: Re-enlisting the negligent

116. *Use of the Reports*

As the pastor receives each report, PLUS ONE, etc., he should circulate copies to the various agencies, departments and ministries that could profit by the suggestions. Thus, the creative work of each Action Group would be made available to the Sunday school, youth groups, etc.; consequently, creative programs may be initiated. In this way, the work of the Alliance for Evangelism can be implemented in all areas of church life.

117. *Burden of Implementation*

Naturally, the burden of implementation will depend on the existing structure and staff of various departments and agencies of the church. The pastor must see that this wealth of material is not sidetracked or placed in some "file 13." The church, the people who participated, the people who prayed—all must be able to see effective changes in all aspects of church programming which reflects both new ways of thinking about evangelism and new ways of doing evangelism.

Effective and workable ideas should also be exchanged with fellow pastors, denominational leaders and Christian friends. Pass the good word around. Involvement works. Concentrated effort works. Christian action works. God's Word works. The power of the Holy Spirit is still available to work through the church and in the lives of individuals to bring about evangelism, Christian service and church growth.

The church has a seven-day-a-week task. Each believer is in full-time Christian service. The work of the church cannot be accomplished with a one-day operation. The building complex ought to be used throughout the week to justify the great cost of construction. The constituency of the church should become a spiritual force within the community. Each individual must find his place of service. Each Christian ought to function as an evangelist and as a missionary every day. The church cannot wait till Sunday and win the world!

APPENDIX A

Alliance for Evangelism Timetable

TASK FORCE ONE

Place these items on the church calendar.

CODE

Quarterly meeting—designated by roman numerals—(I-IV)
—Monthly meeting—designated by all caps—(ONE-SIX)
—Biweekly meeting—designated by numbers—(1-18)
—Special sessions—designated by upper/lower number
(One-Three)

Alliance for Evangelism presented to official board of local church.
Alliance for Evangelism announced to entire local church.

ACTION GROUP LEADERS SELECTED
Action Group Leader Training Session One

ACTION GROUP SECRETARIES SELECTED
Action Group Secretaries Orientation Session
Action Group Leaders Training Session Two
Action Group Leaders Training Session Three

ACTION GROUP PARTICIPANTS SELECTED
Coordinating Council Meeting ONE
Alliance for Evangelism I (all participants)
Action Group Participants Orientation Training by Group
Action Group Session 1
Action Group Session 2
Action Group Session 3
Action Group Session 4

Coordinating Council Meeting TWO
Action Group Session 5
Action Group Session 6
Alliance for Evangelism II (all participants)
Action Group Session 7
Action Group Session 8
Coordinating Council Meeting THREE
Action Group Session 9
Action Group Session 10
Action Group Session 11
Action Group Session 12
Coordinating Council Meeting FOUR
Alliance for Evangelism III
Action Group Session 13
Action Group Session 14
Action Group Session 15
Action Group Session 16
Coordinating Council Meeting FIVE
Action Group Session 17
Action Group Session 18
Alliance for Evangelism IV
Coordinating Council Meeting SIX

TASK FORCE TWO BEGINS
Plus One
Plus Two
Plus Three
Plus Four
Plus Five
Plus Six
Plus Seven

APPENDIX B

(duplicate copies for participant's use in Action Group Session)

ACTION GROUP: _____

AREA OF CONCERN: _____

EVALUATION WORK SHEET AND GUIDE TO INNOVATIVE ACTIVITY

Complete this work sheet for each Area of Concern. Remember individual creativity is the key to vitality and progress. Action Group must develop an openness, independent thinking, flexibility, and order based on experience. Individual members should be concerned with both a new way of doing things and a new way of thinking about things.

1. Who is presently responsible for this action? _____

---

2. What is presently being done in this area? _____

---

3. What can this Action Group do to assist or expedite the matter under present arrangements? _____

---

4. What new effort, program or project could be launched to improve progress or success in this area? _____

---

5. Should new or additional people be assigned to this responsibility? _____

6. Should a whole new program be initiated? _____
Assigned to whom? _____

7. What are your recommendations and/or suggestions for accomplishing the objectives of this Area of Concern? _____

Use the back for additional recommendations and/or ideas, thoughts, concerns, burdens, needs, hopes, etc., you have in this general Area of Concern.

APPENDIX C

(duplicate copies for each Action Group session)

ACTION REPORT

Each group secretary is to prepare a summary report of each ACTION GROUP meeting. Copies should be given to leader and pastor.

Time and Place of Meeting:

Members Present:

General Areas of Discussion:

Conclusions:

Specific Recommendations and/or Suggestions:

(Use back for balance of summary)

Time and place of next scheduled meeting: _____

Signed: _____
Action Group Secretary

APPENDIX D

(Make copies for each participant)

ALLIANCE FOR EVANGELISM PARTICIPANT'S PLEDGE

I shall always seek to exhibit the abundant life which Christ has freely given me. I shall strive with personal enthusiasm to inflame the adventurous spirit among those with whom I am privileged to work. I shall cultivate alertness and keep a vibrant voice and bright eye. I shall endeavor to keep myself physically fit and always available, easily approachable, and ready with friendship and Christian concern for everyone. I shall cultivate an inner poise, control my feelings, be slow to anger, and learn to accept criticism graciously. I shall face my weaknesses honestly and always aspire to excellence in my Christian service and testimony. I shall never stop learning and shall avail myself of every advantage for training and self-improvement. I shall seek for new ideas, read in my field of service, and strive to grow mentally and spiritually.

I pledge sincerity without superficiality. I pledge to be natural, consistent, and to exercise patience.

I pledge to manifest the spirit of love, to seek for inward strength from the Word of God, Christian fellowship and prayer.

I pledge to develop a Christian attitude toward myself, my work, my money, and my relationship with others.

I pledge my faithful service to God and to His church.

I pledge consistent involvement in the outreach ministry of evangelism.

_____   _____
Signed   Date

APPENDIX E

Suggested Reading

Anderson, Philip A., *Church Meetings That Matter*. Philadelphia: United Church Press, 1965.

Ayres, Francis O., *The Ministry of the Laity*. Philadelphia: Westminster, 1961.

Augsburger, Myron. *Faith for a Secular Age World*. Waco: Word, 1968.

Bender, Urie. *The Witness*. Scottsdale, Pa: Herald Press, 1965.

Bounds, E. M., *Power Through Prayer*. Grand Rapids: Zondervan, 1962.

Casteel, John L., *Spiritual Renewal Through Personal Groups*. New York: Association Press, 1967.

Coleman, Robert E., *The Master Plan of Evangelism*. Westwood, New Jersey: Revell. 1963.

Coleman, Robert E., *Dry Bones Can Live Again*. Old Tappan, N.J.: Revell, 1969.

Edge, Findley, B., *A Quest for Vitality in Religion*. Nashville: Broadman.

Green, Hollis L., *Why Churches Die*. Minneapolis: Bethany Fellowship, Inc., 1972.

Halverson, Richard C., *How I Changed My Thinking About the Church*. Grand Rapids: Zondervan, 1972.

Haffer, Eric. *The Ordeal of Change*. New York: Harper & Row, 1952.

Lewis, C. S., *Mere Christianity*. New York: MacMillan, 1943.

Marney, Carlyle. *Structures of Prejudice*. Nashville: Abingdon, 1961.

Morris, Colin. *Include Me Out*. Nashville: Abingdon, 1968.

Mullen, Thomas J., *Ghetto of Indifference*. Nashville: Abingdon, 1966.

Neighbour, Jr., Ralph W., *The Seven Last Words of the Church*. Grand Rapids: Zondervan, 1972.

Olford, Stephen F., *The Secret of Soulwinning*. Chicago: Moody Press, 1963.

Paxson, Ruth. *Life on the Highest Plane.* Chicago: Moody, 1928.
Reid, Clyde, *Groups Alive—Church Alive.* New York: Harper & Row, 1969.
Richards, Larry. *A New Face for the Church.* Grand Rapids: Zondervan, 1970.
Rinker, Rosalind. *Prayer—Conversing with God.* Grand Rapids: Zondervan, 1959.
Schaller, Lyle E., *The Impact of the Future.* Nashville: Abingdon, 1969.
Steere, Douglas. *On Beginning From Within.* New York: Harper & Row, 1964.
Trueblood, Elton. *The Incendiary Fellowship.* New York: Harper & Row, 1967.

APPENDIX F

Leader's Sequence Orientation

1. Read *Why Wait Till Sunday?* It serves as an Alliance for Evangelism manual.
2. Follow the 5-Step S-T-A-R-T Action Approach (p. 17).
3. Brief the church staff on the project.
4. Present the Alliance for Evangelism to the official body of the church so they may fully understand the plans and objectives.
5. Orient the entire church constituency using church publications, public announcements, preaching and personal contact. (Order additional copies of *Why Wait Till Sunday?*)
6. Select the seven Action Group leaders and structure three training sessions for them. Before the training sessions, prepare all materials. Mimeograph or quick copy the Evaluation Work Sheet and Guide to Innovative Activity (Appendix B) and the Action Report (Appendix C). Church staff members should attend all training sessions. In the first session, following the orientation, discuss the choice of secretaries and participants. Make a suggested list.
7. Choose Action Group secretaries and plan an orien-

tation session for them. The secretaries may be included in the second and third session with the Action Group leaders, but not the first session.

8. Schedule a meeting of the Coordinating Council following the training and orientation sessions. This includes the pastor, seven Action Group leaders and seven Action Group secretaries. Here make final decisions concerning the list of all participants making up the full strength Task Force ONE of the Alliance for Evangelism.

9. (1) Seek to involve all participants into Action Groups. Divide the list of participants into the seven Action Groups. (2) Place from three to seven in each group. (Strive to achieve a full-strength force of seven on each group.) Use teens, young marrieds, and older adults. Be certain to have a good age mix on each group. Involve everyone. All regular people who are not selected as Action Group participants should be divided into prayer support groups. The prayer support groups may function under the guidance and leadership of Action Group FIVE.

10. Notify the participants of their selection and set a date for the first Alliance for Evangelism—I (AFE-I) meeting of all participants.

11. Convene Coordinating Council Meeting ONE. Plan a presentation for (AFE-I) and schedule the eighteen Action Group work sessions for the church calendar. Mimeograph or quick copy additional supplies of Evaluation Work Sheet (Appendix B), the Action Report (Appendix C), and the Participant's Pledge (Appendix D) before this meeting.

12. Conduct Alliance for Evangelism—I (AFE-I) for all participants. Challenge the group for a total effort. Action Group leaders along with the pastor and staff should demonstrate excitement and positive attitudes about the prospects for new ways of thinking about evangelism and ways of doing evangelism.

13. Each Action Group leader should structure one orientation or training session for the participants in his group. He should use the information and materials used in his orientation and training sessions. Evaluation Work

Sheets (Appendix B) are needed for each person for every area of concern discussed by the Action Group.

14. Each Action Group leader should conduct four Action Group sessions (Action Group Sessions 1-4) and proceed with the Action Group work sheet process and report structure.

15. Following Action Group Session 4, the Coordinating Council Meeting TWO should meet to evaluate the progress, consider implementation, and receive encouragement and assistance from the pastor. Add additional participants to weak groups to replace anyone who may have dropped out. Strive for a full-strength force.

16. Each Action Group leader should conduct two more Action Group sessions (Action Group Sessions 5, 6) to continue their work before AFE-II meets.

17. Alliance for Evangelism—II (AFE-II) meets to encourage all participants. A general atmosphere of progress and development should dominate the meeting.

18. Each Action Group leader should conduct two Action Group sessions (Action Group Sessions 7, 8) to continue their work.

19. The Coordinating Council Meeting THREE should assemble and evaluate progress. Check attendance at Action Group sessions. If attendance is weak in any area, add support to that Action Group. Strive for a full-strength force.

20. Each Action Group leader should conduct four Action Group Sessions 9-12 to continue their work.

21. Coordinating Council Meeting FOUR should report and evaluate the work of the Action Groups. Also plan for Alliance for Evangelism—III.

22. AFE-III is to encourage all participants to continue their work. Implementation of evangelism in individual lives should be emphasized.

23. Each Action Group leader should conduct four Action Group Sessions 13-16 to continue their work.

24. Coordinating Council Meeting FIVE should prepare for the final sessions of the Action Groups.

25. Action Group leaders should conduct the final two

Action Group Sessions 17, 18 to complete their work.

26. AFE-IV is a final meeting of all participants to express appreciation for service and commend accomplishments. The great unfinished task of implementing evangelism in all aspects of church life should be emphasized. The work of Task Force TWO should be explained to all participants.

27. Coordinating Council Meeting SIX should select seven participants, one from each Action Group, to add to the Coordinating Council to form Task Force TWO. This makes twenty-one lay persons to serve with the pastor for the implementation process.

28. Task Force TWO is to sort and classify all ideas and suggestions and prepare plus reports in the seven areas of the Action Groups work.

29. The seven reports are to be circulated throughout the leadership to spark new approaches to outreach programming.

30. Participants in the Alliance for Evangelism should continually strive for new ways of thinking about evangelism and new ways of doing evangelism. Life-style evangelism is the goal.

www.ingramcontent.com/pod-product-compliance
Lightning Source LLC
LaVergne TN
LVHW011426080426
835512LV00005B/284